Dye Method: Blended Spot Dyes

Contents

1. **Begin Your Journey into Dyeing - 1**
2. **Getting Started: What You Need to Know Before You Dye - 4**
   - General Dyeing Guidelines - 4
   - Selecting the Right Dye - 5
   - Selecting the Right Colors - 6
   - Dyeing with Acid Dyes - 10
   - Dyeing with Direct Dyes - 11
3. **Stocking a Dye Kitchen - 12**
   - Setting Up a Dye Kitchen - 13
   - Heat Sources - 15
4. **Dipping into the Dye Pot (Before You Dive In!) - 17**
5. **Diving into the Dye Pot - 19**
   - Pot Dyeing/Abrash Dyeing - 19
   - Dip Dyeing with a Single Color - 23
   - Double-Color Dip Dye - 28
   - Spot Dyeing: Beautifully Blended and Spotty - 33
   - Casserole Spot Dyeing - 42
   - Swatch Dyeing (No Jars Required) - 48
   - Snow/Ice Dyeing - 52
   - Yarn Dyeing - 56
   - Dyeing Antique - 60

Contents (cont.)

6. Alternative Methods of Dyeing Wool - 62
- Dyeing Wool with Clothing Linings - 62
- Marbleizing Wool with Recycled and As-Is Solid-Colored Wools - 64
- Removing Color from Wool - 66

7. Easy Techniques for Unique Effects - 69
- Dump-and-Go Dyeing - 69
- Dry Dyeing— The Lasagna Method - 71
- Dyeing with Kosher Salt - 75

8. How to Make Ugly Wool Pretty - 78

9. What If . . . ? Why Did . . . ? Situations and Solutions - 82

10. Dye Formulas - 86
- Pot Dye/Abrash Dye Formulas - 86
- Dip Dye Formulas - 87
- Spot Dye Formulas - 91
- Casserole Spot Dyeing Formulas - 95
- Snow and Ice Dyeing Formulas - 99
- Yarn Dyeing Formulas - 102
- Imari Formulas - 108

Glossary - 116

Dye Method: Spotty Spot Dyes

1 — Begin Your Journey into Dyeing

You have been rug hooking, appliquéing, hand sewing, quilting, or braiding for quite a while. As a fiber artist, you want to take the next step and begin to dye your own wool. What a wonderful, creative time in the dye pots you will have!

This dye book is written for those who have never dyed but want to try their hand in the dye pot with success, those who have dyed but stepped away and want to get back to their dye pots, and those who have been dyeing but want to expand their repertoire. And the book will have hints and helps for those of you who have not been satisfied with what is coming out of your dye pots.

I cover everything from A to Z, beginning with what you need to stock your dye kitchen, what type of dye kitchen works for your lifestyle, and most importantly, tried and true methods of dyeing. I want you to be successful in your dye pots, and with these dye recipes and dyeing tricks you will be.

It is my hope that you will use this dye book as your "go-to reference" when you need to dye something for an upcoming project, when you want to explore color in the dye pots, and especially when you want to expand your stash with beautifully dyed wool.

My journey into teaching dyeing began many years ago, when I taught dyeing through adult education programs. I would pack my red wagon with all the dyeing essentials and head to the home economics room at a local high school for a four-or six-week course.

As you begin, renew, or expand your journey into dyeing, this book will be your guide, your compass, and your go-to resource—just as if I were standing right there next to you in your dye kitchen!

Some people are intimidated by the idea of dyeing. But take my word for it—dyeing need not be scary! I hope that these pages will help you see that dyeing is fun and can expand your creativity. Let's get started!

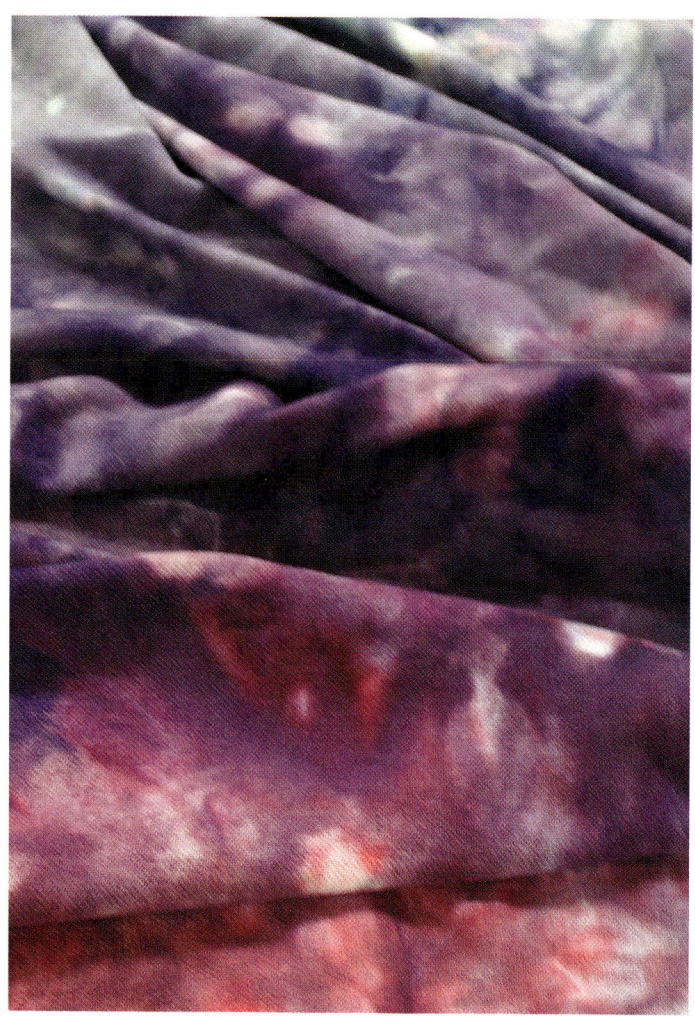

Top Left Dye Method: Spotty Spot Dye

Top Right Dye Methods: Beautifully Blended Spot Dye and Spotty Spot Dye

Right Center Dye Method: Abrash

Bottom Dye Method: Spotty Spot Dye

Top Dye Methods: Abrash, Blended Spot Dye, Spotty Spot Dye, Spotty Spot Dye, Beautifully Blended Spot Dye

Bottom Left Dye Method: Pot Dye

Botto Right Dye Methods: Spotty Spot Dyes and Blended Spot Dyes

Begin Your Journey into Dyeing | 3

2 — Getting Started:
What You Need to Know Before You Dye

General Dyeing Guidelines

- Read all the directions before you start to dye so that you have all the materials readily at hand.

- Make sure the area you use to dye is covered with paper or can be easily cleaned afterward.

- If you are allergic to the dye or to wet wool, use a mask and rubber gloves when handling the dyes. Rubber gloves also protect your fingers from steam burns.

- Never prepare food with the equipment you use to dye.

- Make sure the room has proper ventilation.

- Make sure your wool is clean.

Dyeing is exciting, and some types of dyeing are exacting. Take a little time to read the dyeing instructions carefully . . . and then read them again. Gather your equipment and check the list of what you need a second time. A little preparation can make the whole process easier and more enjoyable, so take the time to prep your area, your wool, and your equipment. You will be glad that you did—it is no fun to be halfway through a process and realize that your dye spoons are still packed away!

If you are a beginner, don't begin dyeing wool for a specific project. It is important to learn how the dyes work and to learn the depth of the color. A good way to start your dyeing journey is to dye all shades of a color first. The Dip Dye Process (page 23) is a great way to begin.

If you are using old garments, be sure to remove the zipper, buttons, waistbands, cuffs, and pleats. Zippers can burn you when you pick the wool up from the hot dye bath and buttons can melt in your dye pot.

Pre-soak your wool in warm water and use a little Lemon Joy to open up the fibers. You can soak your wool for a few hours or overnight.

Keep a notebook and pencil handy to take notes to document the amount of dyes you used, what wools you used, and the end results. This makes it possible for you to repeat the dye formulas you like.

Remember that your wool will always dry a lighter color than what comes out of the dye pot. If the wool does not turn out the color you had hoped for, remember: There are no "failures" in dyeing. You now have a great piece of wool for a future project.

Why Lemon Joy? Won't any detergent work?

Joan Moshimer used Lemon Joy because it contained no petroleum products which would adversely affect how the dye would adhere to the wool, yarn, or fabric. That is still the case today. Joan also felt that Lemon Joy wetted the wool quicker and more efficiently than any other detergent.

SELECTING THE RIGHT DYE

In this book, most of the dyes and names of dyes are acid dyes by W. Cushing & Co. However, any acid dye can be substituted for the W. Cushing acid dyes listed in the formulas.

What is an acid dye? What is a direct dye? What are union dyes? What is the difference?

For many years, W. Cushing's Perfection Dye was a "union" type dye, designed to be suitable for a variety of plant, animal, and synthetic fibers. In response to the changing availability of raw materials and to increase the effectiveness and ease of use of the dyes, they were reformulated about 20 years ago into two types of dye: acid dyes and direct dyes.

Acid dyes are suitable for wool, mohair, and nylon. Direct dyes are better for cottons and cellulose materials, plus linen and rayon. You can dye silk fibers with either, depending on the particular characteristics of the silk.

Dye Types

Acid Dye: use for wool, mohair, and nylon

Direct Dye: use for cottons and cellulose

SELECTING THE RIGHT COLORS

If your color palette is primitive, here are some suggested primitive-color acid dyes:

- Black
- Blue
- Bright Purple
- Bronze
- Bronze Green
- Buttercup Yellow
- Chartreuse
- Dark Brown
- Dark Green
- Egyptian Red
- Gold
- Golden Brown
- Khaki Drab
- Mahogany
- Medium Brown
- Old Gold
- Olive Green
- Plum
- Rust
- Seal Brown
- Silver Gray
- Silver Gray Green
- Terra Cotta
- Turkey Red
- Woodrose

If your color palette is more traditional, here are some suggested traditional-color acid dyes:

- Apricot
- Black
- Blue
- Bronze
- Canary
- Champagne
- Copenhagen Blue
- Ecru
- Garnet
- Gold
- Hunter Green
- Khaki
- Mummy Brown
- Old Gold
- Old Rose
- Orange
- Peacock
- Redgrape
- Reseda Green
- Rose Pink
- Seal Brown
- Silver Gray
- Turkey Red
- Turquoise

Dye Method: Beautifully Blended Spot Dye (Aqualon Pink, Baby Blue, Yellow)

Color Wheel to use with W. Cushing Dyes

Getting Started: What You Need to Know Before You Dye | 7

Color cards for acid dyes and direct dyes show the wide range of dye colors available to you.

Cushing's *Perfection* Direct Dyes
for cellulose fibers, cotton, rayon, basketry reed & other plant fibers

Plum	Navy Blue
Burgundy	Blue
Purple	Light Blue
Violet	Copenhagen Blue
Lavender	Turquoise Blue
American Beauty	Turquoise
Wild Rose	Peacock
Pink	Mint Green
Rose	Bright Green
Crimson	Hunter Green
Scarlet	Green
Cardinal	Dark Green
Egyptian Red	Bronze Green
Terra Cotta	Khaki Drab
Rust	Taupe
Orange	Dark Brown
Buttercup Yellow	Light Brown
Gold	Silver Gray
Yellow	Dark Gray
Canary	Black

This swatch card was produced photographically from cotton swatches dyed at 100% strength. The printing process may alter actual colors.

Dyeing with Acid Dyes

Dyeing with acid dyes is similar to dyeing with union dyes. A dye solution is prepared by measuring the dry dye powder and dissolving it in boiling water. The material to be dyed should be pre-soaked in Lemon Joy dish detergent. The dye bath is prepared in the dye pot by adding water, vinegar, and the dye solution. Water in the pot should be deep enough to cover the material, allowing for stirring.

The term acid refers to the relative pH balance of the dye bath. Therefore, we recommend the use of common white vinegar or citric acid to change that balance. Generally, the amounts required are: one cup of vinegar or one teaspoon of citric acid to a pound of material.

Finally, the dye solution is added to the pot and stirred in thoroughly. Apply heat, and add the pre-wetted material. Continue to stir as the temperature rises to a simmer, then simmer the pot for 30–40 minutes. You will notice that the dye bath will become clearer and clearer as it is exhausted (that is, as the dye solution is taken up into the material).

After the dye bath has exhausted, remove the dye pot from the heat and allow the material to return to cool, rinse the material with cool water, and dry.

Tip!

Different component colors in a dye have different temperature curves. For example, in a green that has a mixture of a yellow and a blue, the blue dyes at a lower temperature than the yellow. This means the blue dye goes into the fabric before the yellow dye does. If the materials are removed from the dye bath prematurely, the result will be uneven or off-shade dyeing. In this example, the results would be bluish because the yellow dye was not taken up. This is why we stress the importance of letting the material simmer for a good while.

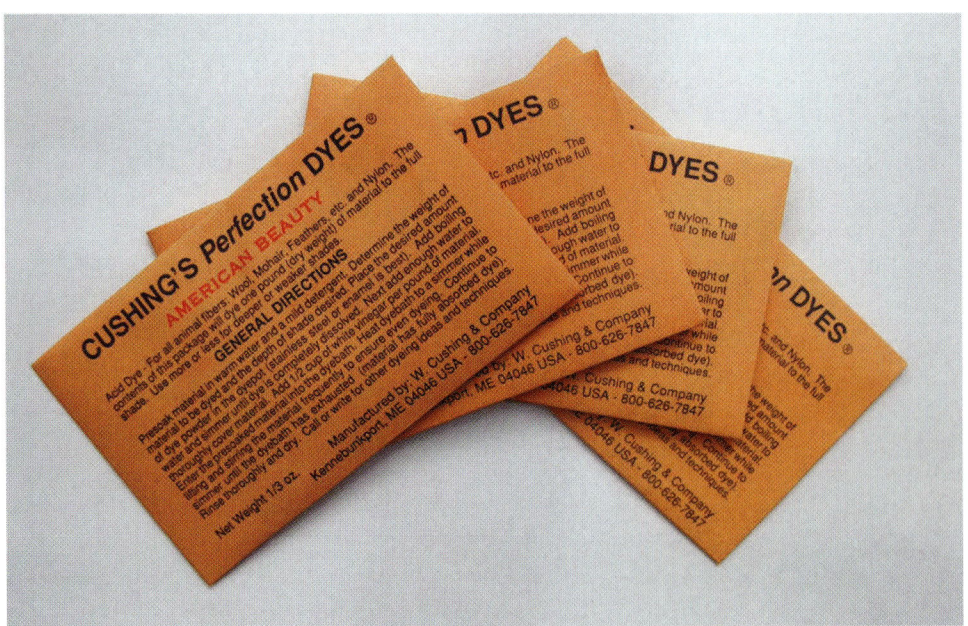

Cushing's acid dyes come in paper envelopes.

Dyeing with Direct Dyes

A wool fiber artist might want to dye some materials other than wool. If this is the case with you, consider using direct dyes. Direct dyes are great for dyeing velvet, cotton, rug warp, monk's cloth, or linen.

Here is another idea: By dyeing the foundation material (the rug warp, monk's cloth, or linen), the rug hooker or puncher does not have to fill in the background. The background can be dyed any color available in direct dyes.

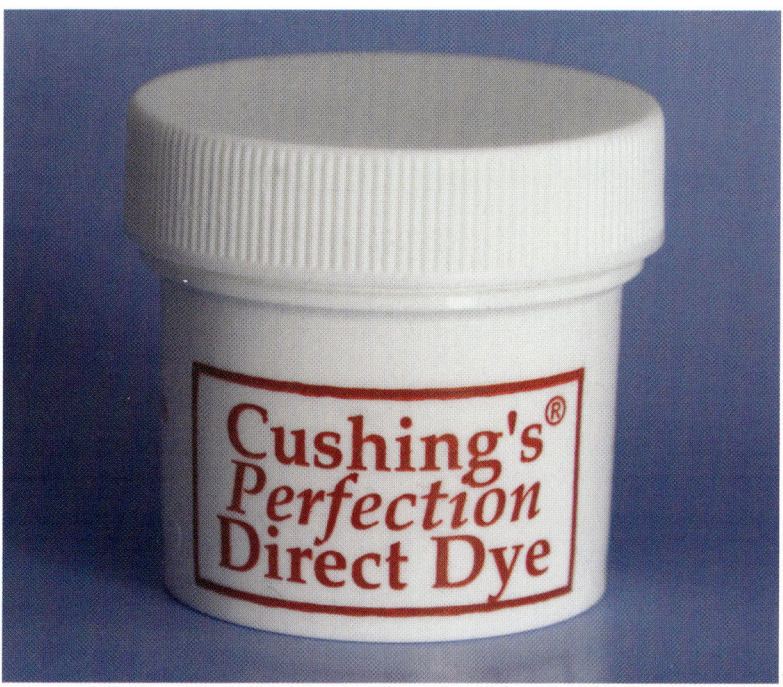

Instructions for Dyeing with Direct Dye

1. Each ½-ounce jar of dye contains enough dye for dying approximately 2 pounds of material. You must weigh your material prior to beginning the process.

2. Use more or less dye for deeper or paler results. (Remember that Cushing's Direct Dyes are intended to use on cotton and other plant fibers, such as basketry material.)

3. Start by thoroughly wetting the materials to be dyed with warm water. This will wash out any sizing or fabric treatment.

4. Dissolve the dry dye in 1 cup of boiling water and set aside.

5. Prepare the dye bath by drawing clean water into a stainless steel, glass, or enamel vessel. Use enough water to completely cover the material, with room enough to allow the liquid to circulate.

6. Place the vessel on heat and allow to simmer.

7. Add salt into the dye pot: Dissolve 4 ounces of common salt for each pound of material and add the dissolved dye that had been set aside. Introduce the material to be dyed to the vessel and bring the pot to a simmer again. Simmer for 20–25 minutes, all the while stirring and agitating to insure even dyeing.

8. Use an after-wash for best colorfastness. You will need 4 ounces of common salt for each pound of material. Add 1 cup of white vinegar. Dissolve in cool water in a separate container; a plastic pail works nicely.

9. Remove dye pot from the heat and rinse material in the after-wash. Let it dry and enjoy the colors.

3 — Stocking a Dye Kitchen

Dye spoons, standard

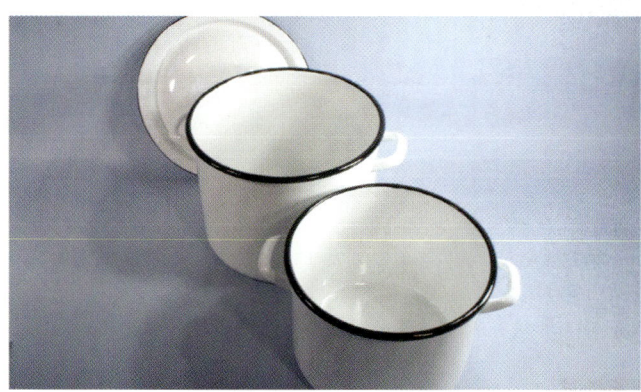
Dye pots

Turkey roaster, electric

Turkey roaster, stove top or oven

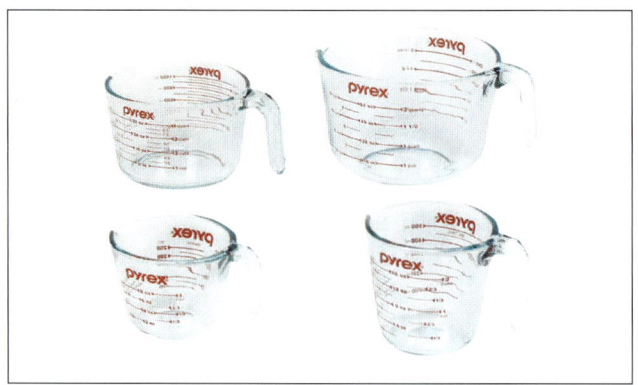
Pyrex measuring cups

Citric acid

What do you need to stock your dye kitchen with the proper equipment and basic utensils? This chapter will give you some suggestions based on how we dye in our very busy dye kitchen.

My #1 Rule: Wear an apron to keep your clothes in good order. Accidents happen.

Glass, enamel, and stainless steel are the best choices for dye equipment as they do not crack under the heat and use. Also, the dye does not stick or clump as it will on plastic; glass, enamel, and stainless steel are easy to clean up. (As when you cook a huge holiday dinner, the cleanup is the worst part! Make it as easy on yourself as you can.)

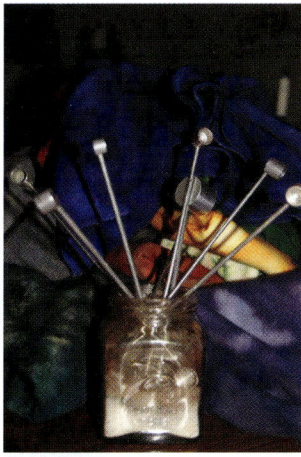

Electric tea kettle

Left: Dye spoons in kosher salt

When we are not dyeing, we keep our dye spoons in a glass jar (an old canning jar) filled with kosher (non-iodized) salt. After we measure our dye, we put the dye spoon in the salt and turn it a few times. This cleans the dye out of the spoon and avoids transferring dye from one pot or one dye session to the next. When the salt in the jar has turned dark with lots of dye, keep it in an airtight glass jar for a great dyeing experience. We'll talk about this super fun dyeing method later. (See chapter 6, page 73.)

Keep pot holders and dish towels within reach so when you pour the boiling water into the glass measuring cup, you can hold onto the tea kettle with a pot holder. If you should spill water or dye on the floor, wipe it up immediately with a dish towel—you don't want to slip!

For quick cleanups: keep a spray bottle with a mix of one part bleach to two parts water.

Keep your measuring cups on a plastic place mat. These are inexpensive, easy to clean, and are disposable after they are too stained to clean.

Keep your dyes in their original envelopes. This keeps the W. Cushing Perfection Dyes stable and away from light. Store your dye envelopes in a plastic tub away from the windows.

Wooden spoons

Setting Up a Dye Kitchen

This is what we have in our dye kitchen at W. Cushing. As you build your own equipment stash, consider this list.

Equipment for Setting Up a Dye Kitchen

- Measuring cups (glass not plastic)
    - 1 cup
    - 2 cups
    - 4 cups
- Enamel pots—2 or 3 different sizes. The best sizes are 4-quart and 8-quart.
- Enamel turkey roaster, with lid
- Large rectangular stainless-steel pans (for spot dyeing)
- Long utensils and tongs to stir the wool
- Wooden spoons
- Electric tea kettle
- Metal measuring spoons
- Lemon Joy (ONLY)
- Bluettes rubber gloves or disposable gloves
- Kosher (non-iodized) salt in a glass jar
- Distilled white vinegar (from the supermarket)
- Citric acid (commercial grade)
- Aluminum foil
- Cleanup spray, water with bleach
- Paper towels, newspaper
- Notebook and pencil
- Apron to protect your clothing
- Pot holders
- Dish towels
- Plastic place mats

Hints!

- Alternative to measuring cups: you can use mason jars instead of measuring cups. Mark the jars on the side with ounce marks. With jars, you can seal the unused dye for later use.

- Alternative to measuring spoons: you can use the metal baking spoons marked Smidgen, Pinch, Dash, and Tad (see table below for conversion).

- Wooden spoons. Purchase inexpensive spoons at a dollar store. You will need to change them frequently because they stain and can transfer color from one dye pot to another. We change them once a month.

- If you are having trouble finding good enamel pots, start with an electric turkey roaster, 18 quarts. These can control the heat and provide a lid instead of using aluminum foil. We have found the Oster brand electric turkey roaster stands up to the wear and tear of dyeing.

- Tea kettle: a traditional stovetop tea kettle can be used. However, an electric tea kettle heats the water to the correct heat to mix the dyes.

- Remember: store your dye equipment away from your everyday kitchen utensils and **never, ever** use any of these tools for cooking food.

Measuring Spoon Equivalents

- **Smidgen** – 1/32 tsp.
- **Pinch** – 1/16 tsp.
- **Dash** – 1/8 tsp.
- **Tad** – 1/4 tsp.

Heat Sources

Why is the source of heat for your dye pots so important? You need a heat source that is consistent—a reliable temperature so that when you dye you can repeat the dye method for similar results.

You also want a safe heat source—one that will not break, catch fire, or burn your dye pots. If possible, it should be dedicated to dyeing exclusively and not perform double duty as your cooking stove.

Whether you use a gas or electric stove, be sure to have a good vent over the stove. You will want to vent the steam out of the dye kitchen.

HEATING SOURCES FOR A PERMANENT DYE KITCHEN

Gas, propane, or natural gas stove

The best source is a simple gas, propane, or natural gas stove. Why a simple stove? As my grandmother always said, "You don't need a fancy stove to be a good cook." The same applies for dye kitchens! What makes a simple gas stove so great?

- A simple stove does not have a lot of bells and whistles, such as a convection oven, different heat settings, or different configurations of the metal plates.
- A four-burner gas stove is perfect and not too expensive.
- The stove is easy to keep clean (you should clean your stove with a bleach cleaner at the end of each dyeing session). The grates will build up a residue from the dye pots over time, so they should be cleaned to remove the residue.
- It is easy to control the heat by adjusting the flame, giving even, consistent heat which then allows for even, consistent dyeing.

Electric stove

An electric stove that is simple and has burners that are easy to clean is another good choice. If you are not familiar with or comfortable with a gas stove, an electric stove with burners is the next best thing. Once again, keep it simple.

- You don't need a convection oven or a lot of buttons or different temperature controls. You want a stove that makes it easy to clean and dye.
- On any stove, the burner has to heat up to the proper temperature. This takes longer on an electric stove. Be mindful of this extra time and that it may take longer to heat your dye pots.
- Be sure your electric burners can be removed and easily cleaned or replaced. The residue will build on them from your dye pots.

Never use a glass top electric stove for a dye kitchen. Your dye pots filled with water and wool are very heavy to lift and move. Should one slip from your hands and land on the glass top of the stove, it will shatter the glass top. Also, when water splashes onto a glass top electric stove from the dye pots, it creates an instant residue. This residue has to be cleaned with the special cleaner for glass stoves (normally comes with the stove) or it will create a spot that does not heat properly, leaving you with uneven heat.

HEATING SOURCES FOR A PORTABLE DYE KITCHEN

A portable dye kitchen allows you to store what you need on a shelf in your basement or garage. When you are going to dye, you grab the equipment off the shelf and set up your dye kitchen. As always, if dyeing inside, be sure that you have good ventilation via a fan or vent.

> **Tip!**
>
> While almost all of the turkey roasters have black pans, it will not take you long to realize you have to pull the wool out of the pan to see the color. (White dye pots are always best as they allow you to see the color as you are dyeing it.)

Electric turkey roaster

A good size electric turkey roaster is 18 quarts. You can dye up to 1¾ yards of wool or two skeins of yarn in it. Why is an electric turkey roaster so wonderful for a portable dye kitchen?

- Simplicity. You simply put paper or an old cloth down on the table and then plug in the turkey roaster, fill it with water, and you are ready to begin!
- Control. You can control the temperature. The electric turkey roaster comes with a lid to keep the dye bath from boiling away and keep the steam in the dye pot.
- Ease of cleaning. Once you have finished dyeing for the day and the pan in the turkey roaster has cooled, you wash out the pan with dish detergent and water. Be sure to rinse well so there is no dye residue that could transfer to your next dyeing session.
- Storage. You can store your measuring cups, dye spoons, citric acid, and dyes (in an airtight container) inside the turkey roaster. Then simply put your turkey roaster on the shelf until you are ready to dye again.
- Cost. Most cost under $50.00. We have found the Oster brand to work the best and stand up to the rigors of dyeing.

Outdoor grill

- A gas or electric grill is not built to withstand the weight of a dye pot filled with water and wool. If the grill is not heavy duty, the weight of the dye pot may crease or bend it.
- The heat controls to the grill are not very precise and so may give inconsistent heat. You don't want to burn the dye pots nor do you want to wait for a long time to have the dye pots heat up.
- Just as when grilling, if the dye pots boil over, it will cause fire flashes which could lead to a fire.
- As with any of your dye equipment, never cook your food on the same heat source you dye on.

Gas burners

One- and two-burner outdoor gas burners are available in a variety of configurations. Gas burners are to be used exclusively outdoors, connected to a propane tank.

The advantage to using the gas burners outside is that you do not have to ventilate while you dye, and you can dye in a larger pot which means more wool dyed at one time!

The dye pots on a gas burner have to be monitored closely as they tend to boil quickly. Watch the water level: keep ample water in the dye pots so the wool does not burn. The best dye method if you use gas burners is the pot dye method.

4 — Dipping into the Dye Pot
(Before You Dive In!)

Before diving into the dye pot, many fiber artists like to dip into the dye pot first. By dipping into the dye pot, you test the waters—and learn a lot along the way.

Many first-time dyers or those who have been out of the dye pot for some time are intimidated by dyeing, worried that they will produce dyed wool that looks like mud (when they wanted grass), or that they will never be able to understand the directions and dye methods.

Never fear. Remember, dyeing need not be scary. Take a look at these procedures and you to will be ready to dip into the dye pot!

What You Need

- Wool: ¼ yd., wet and soaked with Lemon Joy
- Acid dye: your favorite color
- Four-quart pot
- Dye spoon: ¼ tsp.
- One 2-cup glass measuring cup
- Electric kettle
- White vinegar
- Heat source of your choice
- Wooden spoon
- Rectangular pan (for wool to cool)
- Tongs
- Wooden spoons

We always start our dye workshops with this simple dye process. But dyeing is contagious: those skeptical of dyeing, or those who just planned to observe, soon have a dye spoon in one hand and are selecting dye colors with the other.

Simple dyeing method:
Take a quarter yard of wool (18" x 30") and soak it in warm water with Lemon Joy for about 30 minutes.

While your wool is soaking, fill a 4-quart pot halfway with water, and bring it to a simmer; in my dye kitchen, a simmer means no bubbles, just steam rising off the pot. Then select your favorite color. Let's pick Robin's Egg Blue.

Measure ¼ tsp. of the dye into a 2-cup glass measuring cup. Add boiling water from a tea kettle and stir until the dye is completely dissolved. This mixture is your dye solution.

By now your water is simmering in the pot. Pour your dye solution into the simmering water, stir, and add ⅛ cup of vinegar. Stir again. Now you have a dye bath.

Drop your presoaked wet wool in the dye pot. Stir clockwise twice, then stir counterclockwise twice, with a wooden spoon.

Set the timer for 20 minutes. After 20 minutes, check your wool and dye bath. If the water is clear, pull the wool out and set it in a pan or in the sink for about 15 minutes. Rinse with cool water and dry on a clothesline or in your dryer.

That is all there is to it. See how easy it is to dye your first piece of wool?

Hints!

Still too complicated for you? Here are a few suggestions:

- Join a friend who dyes for a day of dyeing. You act as her assistant and observe what she is doing. I guarantee that soon you will be in your own dye pots!

- Take a mini class at a local adult education center or sign up for a beginning dye workshop near you.

- Go online. There are many podcasts and videos about dyeing wool. Sit down, take notes, and observe the process. While you are not actually dipping into the dye pot, you are gaining confidence by watching an expert create lovely wool.

5 — Diving into the Dye Pot
Pot Dyeing/Abrash Dyeing

Abrashed wool with great movement

This is a great way to begin dyeing. It is so versatile and simple—especially great for your Ugly Wool. We all have some in our stashes, don't we? So let's turn that ugly wool into beautiful wool by pot dyeing. And you can overdye textures you do not think you will use as is. It is amazing what you can do in a simple pot dye session.

If you are dyeing a new color, or if you want to test the color of a dye formula, you can do that with a pot dye. This allows you to confirm the color before dyeing yards of wool the wrong color.

Mottled wool, stirred a bit too much

The pot dye method creates an abrash effect. The abrash effect is a mottled, unevenly dyed wool. Abrashed wool creates movement, depth of color, and a mottled effect when hooked. You will see darks and lights of the color in the same piece of wool, all in a mottled fashion. Abrashed, mottled wool is fabulous to hook with—the wool does a lot of the work for you.

By combining solid wools, white wool, and textured wool in the same dye pot, you will get a wonderful array of dyed wools to use for trees, grasses, geometrics, and Orientals. And, since they came from the same dye pot, you know that they will go together. The more textures and solids you mix in a pot, the more varied the wool will be.

How would you use abrashed wool?

- Pot dyed wool is great for creating backgrounds or mixing dyed wool with textures for an awesome background.

- Use it with Oriental patterns because the abrash effect creates a worn look when hooked.

- Use it for skies, from stormy to blue, so the skies have movement.

- Pot dyed/abrashed wool makes wonderful water, from oceans to babbling brooks.

- Hook hills and mountains, in any season.

- Hook vintage flowers and leaves.

- Hook clothing with this dyed wool; the dark wrinkle lines are built right into the abrashed wool.

The best size dye pot to start pot dyeing with (unless you are using an electric turkey roaster) is a 4-quart pot.

Once you master pot dyeing with a single dye solution, try using multiple colors. For example, you might start with a dye solution of Old Gold, then pour in a second dye solution of Golden Brown. The possible combinations are endless.

Tip!

Pot dyed wool combines nicely with wool dyed in the dip dye method or the wools you dye with one of our alternative dye methods. For example, if you have dip dyed wool in Redgrape for the vein of a leaf, you can pot dye Bronze Green for the leaf.

What You Need

- Wool: solid and textures, for a total of no more than a yard, soaked in warm water with Lemon Joy

- Acid dye(s)

- Enamel or stainless steel 4-quart pot

- Dye spoon: ¼ tsp. and ½ tsp.

- 4-cup glass measuring cup

- Citric acid or white vinegar

- Heat source of your choice

- Wooden spoon

- Rectangular pan for cooling

Step-by-Step Abrash Dyeing Instructions

Crowded pot

Stirring to mottle the wool

1. Pre-soak your wool in warm water with a little Lemon Joy to open up the fibers. You can soak your wool for a few hours or overnight.

2. The size of the pot you need depends on the amount of wool you wish to dye. You can use your turkey roaster as a pot for this method; use no more than ¾ yd. of wool in a turkey roaster.

3. Fill your pot halfway with water.

4. Heat the pot of water to steaming, not to a full boil. If you see bubbles in your pot of water, you need to turn down the heat.

5. Add the soaked wool to the pot; the water should cover the wool. If it does not, add more boiling water.

6. Put ½ tsp. dye into 4 cups boiling water. This is your dye solution.

7. Pour the dye solution into the steaming pot of water and stir only once with a wooden spoon. This is your dye bath.

8. The more you stir, the less mottled the wool will be. Let the wool simmer for 12 to 15 minutes, until the dye bath is almost clear.

9. Add ¼ cup of white vinegar or ¼ tsp. of citric acid; remove after 3 to 5 minutes. The dye bath water should be clear.

10. Remove the wool from the pot and put it into the clean rectangular pan.

11. Rinse your wool in cool water and line dry, or dry in a dryer on the lowest setting.

Side by side for comparison: the wool on the left has movement, the wool on the right was stirred just a bit too much.

Diving into the Dye Pot

Hints!

- To add mottling, use textured wool.

- A crowded pot is a happy pot. A crowded pot will result in more mottling.

- If you are using an electric turkey roaster, the maximum amount of wool to use is ¾ yd.

- Keep your electric tea kettle hot in case you need more hot water quickly.

- It is difficult to reproduce exactly the same color using this dye method. The wools will never be put in the pot exactly the same way, or you might not have exactly the same wools (or the same amounts of those wools). Nevertheless, you will get wool with a similar look, and the wool will hook very similarly and go together well.

- If your dyed wool does not have enough mottling, you may have stirred the pot too much.

- If you are dyeing a large amount of wool for a background, for best results, mix solids and textured.

Dip Dyeing with a Single Color

A dip dyed piece of wool has the darkest to lightest values of one color on one piece of wool, without any hard defining lines. Dip dyed wool gives you a smooth transition of color from one value to the next.

Many rug hookers are unfamiliar with dip dyed wools, which have a special beauty and usefulness in a wide variety of patterns and cuts. Dip dyed wools lend themselves to shading, in many cut sizes, with ease and grace.

For the beginner dyer, dip dyeing wool is easy, fun, and a fabulous way to learn all about the gradations of dye colors.

For dip dyeing, your wool must be wet to absorb the color easily. You do not have to hold the wool straight out, as if it were hanging like clothes on a clothesline. If the wool folds or pleats a bit in your hands, you will be adding even more to the depth of color.

If you are looking for dyed wool that easily combines with textures, a dip dyed wool is perfect. The dip dyed wool could be the maple leaf while you use a texture for the veins. Or you could reverse these and make the leaf the texture and the veins the dip dye.

Remember: if you are hooking scrolls or even geometrics and you feel the motifs need more movement and depth, a dip dyed piece of wool will help!

How Would You Use Dip Dyed Wool?

- Shading in leaves from spring greens to fall golds
- Shading flowers: irises, tulips, lilies, and pansies
- Hooking scrolls or twisted ribbons
- Hooking geometrics
- Animals: fur and feathers

SINGLE COLOR DIP DYE METHOD – WHAT YOU NEED

- Wool (for amount of wool, see #2 on page 26.) wet and soaked in warm water and Lemon Joy.
- Acid dyes
- Enamel or stainless-steel 1- or 2-qt. pot
- Dye spoon: ¼ tsp.
- 2-cup glass measuring cup
- Citric acid or white vinegar
- Heat source of your choice
- Wooden spoon
- Rectangular pan

Step-by-Step Single Dip Dye Instructions

1. Cut the wool in either long skinny quarters (9" x 60") or fat quarters (18" x 30") or half yard pieces (18" x 60"). If you would like a long draw of the color, use the 9" x 60" piece of wool. If you would like a dip dye for flowers or skies, use the half yard pieces. NOTE: if this is your first dip dye, try the 18" x 30" pieces until you get a rhythm.

2. Pre-soak the wool in warm water and use a little Lemon Joy to open up the fibers. You can soak your wool for a few hours or overnight.

3. Bring a pot of water to a steam, not a full boil. The pot should have 8 to 12 cups of water.

4. Put ¼ tsp. of your chosen dye into 2 cups boiling water. This is your dye solution.

5. Add the citric acid (¼ tsp.) or white vinegar (¼ cup) to the dye formula, not to the pot of water. By adding acid to the dye solution, the color will grab evenly and quickly onto the wool. This is a called a quick set dye.

6. Pour the dye solution into the steaming pot of water and stir thoroughly with a wooden spoon. This is the dye bath.

7. Pick up the wool and carefully hold it over the pot of water.

8. Drop the bottom 3" of the wool into the dye bath, and immediately move the wool up and down. Dip it 8 to 10 times.

9. Gradually drop more of the wool into the dye bath, still continuously moving the wool up and down (dipping) so there is no hard, solid dye line.

10. Continue dipping, adding increments of wool, until you have reached the top 1-2" of the wool.

11. Take the top 3" and drape it over your wooden spoon. Now quickly dip the top of the wool (the not-yet-dyed section) into the dye, one or two times, to fill in the lightest value.

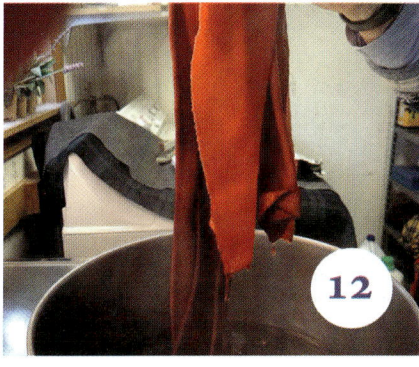 

12. Remove the dip dyed wool from the pot into a separate clean pan. A good pan to use is a square enamel or stainless-steel pan.

13. Rinse your wool in cool water and line dry, or dry in a dryer on the lowest setting.

Diving into the Dye Pot | 27

Double-Color Dip Dye

A double-color dip dye is wool that begins with dip dyed wool in one color and ends with dip dyed wool in another color. For example, the wool might change from purple to yellow, or from red to peach.

DOUBLE-COLOR DIP DYE METHOD – WHAT YOU NEED

- Wool: for amount of wool see #2 on page 31, wet and soaked in warm water and Lemon Joy
- Acid dyes in the colors of your choosing
- Enamel or stainless-steel 1- or 2-qt. pot. You will need two pots.
- Dye spoon: ¼ tsp.
- Two 2-cup glass measuring cups, one for each color
- Citric acid or white vinegar
- Heat source of your choice
- Wooden spoon
- Rectangular pan

Double color dip dye setup

How to control the wool lengths as you dip dye

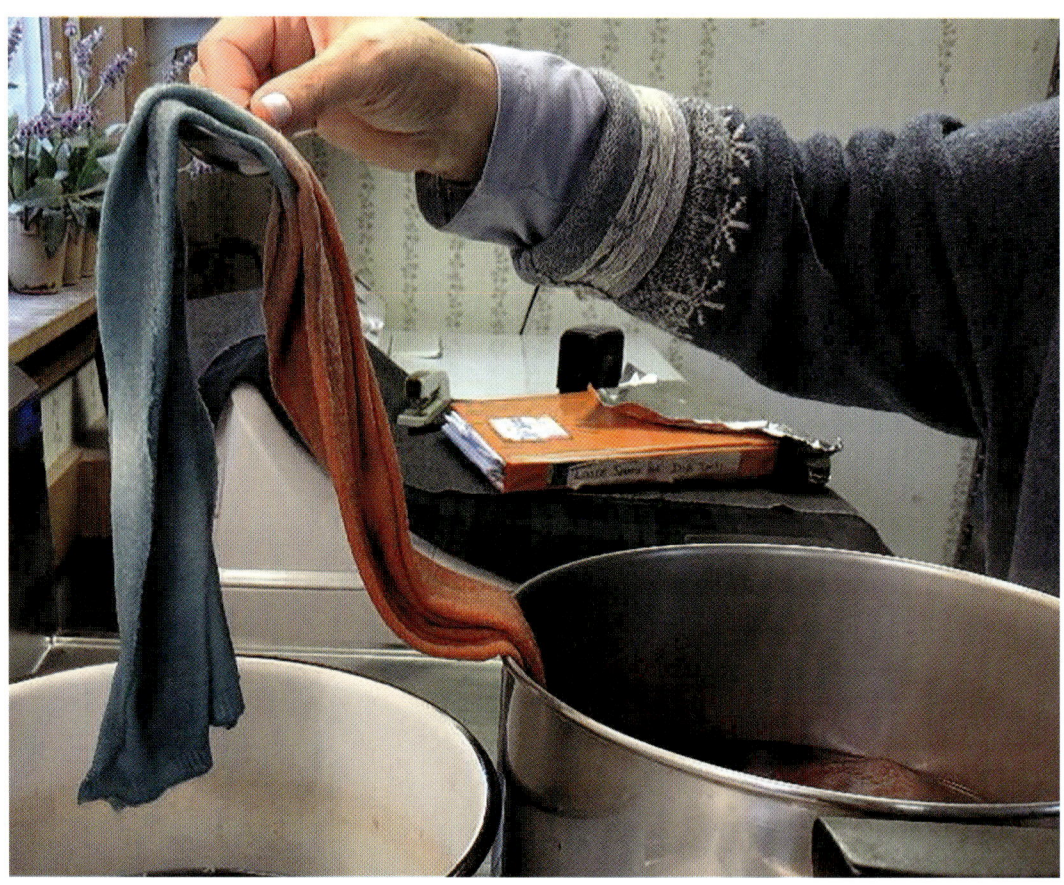

Gorgeous wool in a double dip dye

STEP-BY-STEP DOUBLE COLOR DIP DYE INSTRUCTIONS

1. Cut the wool in either long skinny quarters (9" x 60") or fat quarters (18" x 30") or half yard pieces (18" x 60").

2. Pre-soak the wool in warm water with a little Lemon Joy to open up the fibers. Soak the wool for a few hours or overnight.

3. Bring two pots of water to a steam, not to a full boil. The pots should each have 8 to 12 cups of water.

4. Mix the first dye color in a glass measuring cup (4-cup measuring cup is best).

5. Add the citric acid (¼ tsp.) or white vinegar (¼ cup) to the dye formula, not to the pot of water. This is called a quick set dye. The dye will grab quickly to the wool.

6. Mix the second dye color as you mixed the first. Add citric acid or vinegar.

7. Pour the first dye bath into the first steaming pot of water. Stir thoroughly with a wooden spoon.

8. Pour the second dye bath into the second steaming pot of water and stir thoroughly with a different wooden spoon.

9. Drop the bottom 3" of the wool into the dye pot with your main color, and immediately begin dipping the wool up and down.

10. Gradually drop more of the wool into the dye bath, still continuously moving the wool up and down (dipping) so there is no hard, solid dye line.

11. Continue dipping until you have reached the top 4" of the wool.

12. Take the top 6" (allowing overlap) and drape it over your wooden spoon.

13. Quickly dip the top of the wool (the undyed section) one or two times in the second dye pot to fill in and overlap the first dip dyed color.

14. Remove the dip dyed wool from the pot into a separate clean pan.

15. Rinse the wool in cool water and line dry or dry in a dryer on the lowest setting.

Hints!

- The best wool to use for dip dyeing is a white or cream wool so that the graduation of color is smooth and crisp.

- If you want to use colored wool, use only light blue, yellow, or mint green.

- Keep your wooden spoon handy. You will need it for the final dip so that you do not burn your fingers or make the top of the dip dye too dark.

- Keep the first 3" of wool in the pot throughout the entire process. That will assure that you achieve the darkest value of the color at the base of the wool.

- If you have hard lines that delineate the different values of color, it means you did not dip the wool quickly enough. The dip dyed wool will still shade.

- If your dye bath still has color, you can dip dye another piece of wool and continue on dyeing until the dye bath is clear. This will give you a wide range of values of one color.

- Do not dip dye more than one piece of wool at a time. If you hold two pieces of wool as you dip, one piece of wool will fold too much creating creases, or one piece will have harsh lines of color.

- The double color dip dye method works best with a rich dye for the base (such as Redgrape, Mulberry, Olive Green, or Seal Brown) and a lighter color dye for the top (such as Buttercup Yellow, Chartreuse, Orchid, or Baby Blue).

Tip!

How much wool should I dip dye?

Remember that you will need wool about four times longer than the space you are planning to hook with dip dyed wool. For instance, if you are hooking a twisting ribbon that measures 6" long, you will need a piece of dip dyed wool about 24" long.

Spot Dyeing

Spot dyeing has long been called the "fashion wool" for rug hookers. Spot dyed wools are beautiful before they are cut and hooked. They can resemble hand-painted pieces of art, with highlights and shading, all in one piece. Sometimes it feels like a shame to cut into these luscious pieces.

Spot dyed wool normally uses three colors; the main color, the secondary color, and the accent color. By correctly combining the three colors, you will have a dyed piece of wool that has depth, interest, and movement. Spot dyed wool combines nicely with textures to add depth, definition and direction to your rug hooking.

Choosing Colors for a Spot Dye

The main color should be the color that you wish to see the most, and the darkest of the three colors. Your main color sets the tone for the entire spot dye.

For example, if you are spot dyeing for a hillside of green that has multiple tones you might start with Bronze Green.

The secondary color should blend with your main color, and it should be a strong color to stand up to your main color but not overpower it. The secondary color is sometimes the hardest color to choose. Remember: less intense is better. The secondary color should be one that you like as it will appear almost as often as the main color. A secondary color that blends with Bronze Green (and is strong enough to stand up to Bronze Green) is Aqua.

Your accent color should be chosen to highlight both your main color and secondary color and it should be the lightest of the three colors. When choosing the highlight, think of a color that will add light to the other two colors, like sunshine on a hillside. In this instance, the highlight color is Mint Green.

Spot dyed wool can be a beautiful blend of three colors or it can be a "spotty" dyed wool of three colors. The two techniques for spot dyeing wool are quite different, producing very different wool.

The beautiful blend spot dye produces a watercolor wool that looks hand painted. The transition of colors is soft. It is perfect for impressionistic pictorials or realistic animals. This method takes time, patience, and practice. You can hook "highlights" on the parts of the design that you want to accentuate and shadow the other areas. Let yourself go and it's a safe bet you will be surprised and delighted.

The other type of spot-dyed dyeing gives you spotty dyed wool. This wool has the original color of the wool showing between the spots of other colors. The colors are distinctive and when it is hooked, it can be great for accents in rugs, animals, and flowers, and for rug borders. If you do not want the wool to be spotty, you will need to take a bit more time when blending the colors together.

Spot dye your favorite color combination over white wool, cream wool, pink wool, and light blue wool. By using colors such as lavender, light blue, pink, yellow, or camel, your spot dyed wool will have more depth and less chance of white wool showing through. Create a sampler of a specific color combination. You can create a complete palette of colors for one rug. You will have wool that will work beautifully as a background or different elements in a pictorial.

Beautifully Blended Spot Dye Method – 4-Part Spot Dye

Wool ready to dye

Dye bath equipment

*Dye bath set up, dye prepared.
Please note the window for natural light*

Correct application of first color

Correct application of second color

Dye pan with two colors applied

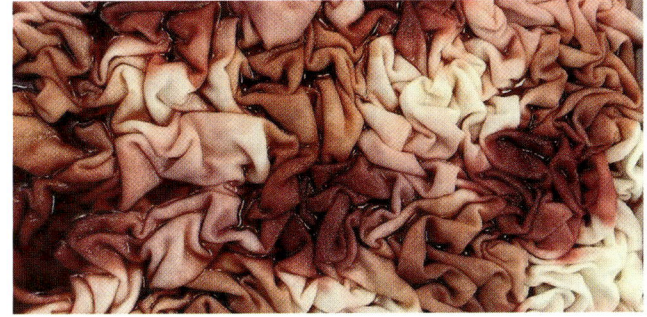

Dye pan with three colors applied

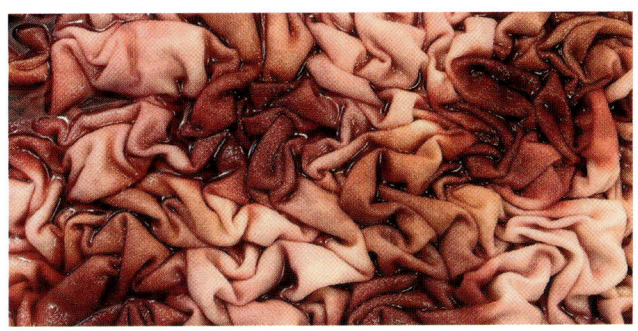

Dye pan with four colors applied

Diving into the Dye Pot | 35

Beautifully Blended Spot Dyeing Method – What You Need

- Wool: 1 yd. plus 2", wet and soaked in warm water with Lemon Joy

- Acid dyes

- Enamel or stainless-steel flat pan, 16" x 24" or smaller

- Dye spoon: ½ tsp.

- Three 2-cup glass measuring cups

- Metal tablespoon

- Citric acid or white vinegar

- Heat source

- Wooden spoon

- Rectangular pa

- Electric tea kettle

STEP-BY-STEP BEAUTIFULLY BLENDED SPOT DYE INSTRUCTIONS

1. Pre-soak your wool (1 yd. plus 2") in warm water with a little Lemon Joy to open up the fibers. You can soak your wool for a few hours or overnight.

2. Let the wool drain in the sink. Do not squeeze out excess water.

3. You will need boiling water in step 9. So be sure to turn the kettle on now so that it is boiling when you need it.

4. Prepare the main color dye solution: In the first 2-cup glass measuring cup, mix ½ tsp. of the main color with 2 cups boiling water. Stir well (every granule of dye must be dissolved before proceeding).

5. Prepare the second color dye solution: In the second 2-cup glass measuring cup, mix ½ tsp. of your second color with 2 cups of boiling water and stir well.

6. Prepare the third color dye solution: In the third 2-cup glass measuring cup, mix ½ tsp. of the highlight color with 2 cups boiling water and stir well.

7. Take your wet wool and, without wringing it out, place it in the bottom of the large flat pan. It will be much too large to fit flat in the pan, so with both hands, distribute the cloth as evenly as you can. Take a few minutes with this step. It will be wrinkled; this wrinkling will make beautiful patterns when you apply the dyes. The smaller the pan is, the more time you will have to take to tuck the wool down and distribute it as evenly as possible. Take your time with this important step.

8. With a tablespoon, spoon the main color onto the wool, in spots about the size of a medium apple and about 2" to 3" apart. (You will use about 1 to 1¼ cups of the dye solution). Use the back of the tablespoon to blend the main color spots into the wool.

9. Carefully pour 4 cups of plain hot boiling water over those spots.

10. With the tablespoon, spoon the secondary color onto the wool in the spaces next to the main color. Use the back of the tablespoon to blend the main color with the secondary color so they mix and all the wool between them is covered with dye solution (you will use a little over 1½ cups of the dye solution).

11. With the tablespoon, carefully spoon the highlight color onto the wool in the blank spaces or blended spaces between the main and secondary colors. Using the back of the spoon, blend all colors together carefully so that no white or cream wool shows. Take your time; be sure the entire piece of wool is covered before you go to the next step.

12. Pour ½ cup of vinegar over the entire pan of wool.

13. Let the wool simmer (not boil) for 25 to 30 minutes or until the water under the dyed wool is clear. Important: Do not let the water evaporate from the pan or you will burn your wool.

14. Remove the spot dyed wool from the pot into a separate clean pan. Let the wool sit for 10 to 15 minutes to cool.

15. Rinse your wool in cool water, not cold water. Cold water will shock the wool and could cause the wool to felt. Line dry, or dry in a dryer on the lowest setting.

"Spotty" Spot Dyeing

"Spotty" dyed wool has the original color of the wool showing between the spots of color. The wool shown in this sequence definitely has three spots of color that are clear and concise.

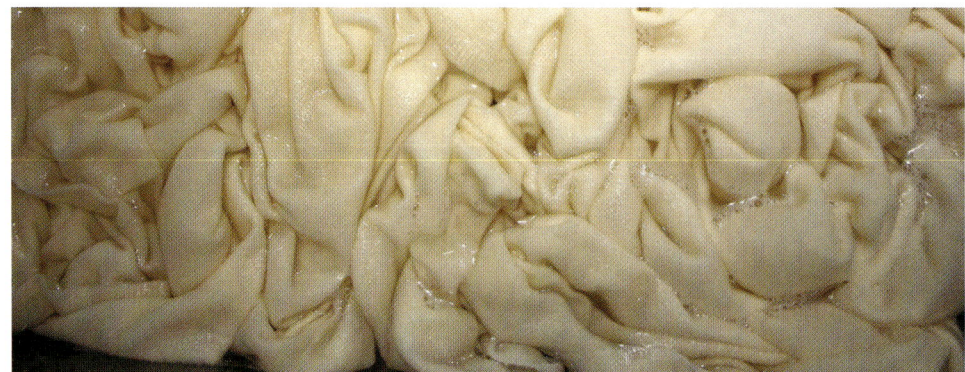

Soaking the wool

Traditional dye bath for spotty dye

Wool with one color applied

Wool with two colors applied

Wool with three colors applied

Spot dye in the pan—dark colors

Spot dye in the pan—light colors

Spot dyed wool

"Spotty" Spot Dyeing Method – What You Need

- Wool: 1 yard plus 2", wet and soaked in warm water with Lemon Joy

- Acid dyes

- Enamel or stainless-steel flat pan, 16" x 24" or smaller

- Dye spoons: ¼ tsp. and ½ tsp.

- Three 2-cup glass measuring cups

- Metal tablespoon

- Citric acid or white vinegar

- Heat source of your choice

- Wooden spoon

- Rectangular pan

- Electric kettle

Step-by-Step "Spotty" Spot Dye Instructions

1. Pre-soak your wool (one yard plus 2") in warm water and use a little Lemon Joy to open the fibers. You can soak your wool for a few hours or overnight.

2. Let the wool drain in the sink. Do not squeeze out excess water.

3. Prepare the main color dye solution: In the first 2-cup glass measuring cup, mix ½ tsp. of your main color with 2 cups boiling water. Stir well (every granule of dye must be dissolved before proceeding).

4. Prepare the second color dye solution: In the second 2-cup glass measuring cup, mix ½ tsp. of your second color with 2 cups of boiling water and stir well.

5. Prepare the accent color: In the third 2-cup glass measuring cup, mix ½ tsp. of your highlight color with 2 cups boiling water and stir well.

6. Take your wet wool and, without wringing it out, place it in the bottom of the large flat pan. It will be much too large to fit flat in the pan. So with both hands, distribute the cloth as evenly as you can. Take a few minutes with this step. It will be wrinkled—it is this wrinkling that will make the beautiful pattern when you apply the dyes. The smaller the pan is, the more time you will have to take to tuck the wool down. Distribute it as evenly as possible. Take your time as you do this important step.

7. With a tablespoon, spoon the main color onto the wool, in spots about the size of a medium apple, about 2" to 3" apart. (You will use about 1 to 1¼ cups of the dye solution.) Blend the color into the wool with the back of the tablespoon.

8. Carefully pour 4 cups of plain hot boiling water over the spots you just created.

9. With the tablespoon, spoon the secondary color onto the wool in the spaces next to the main color. Use the back of the tablespoon to blend the main color and the secondary color so they mix; leave some spots of the original base wool showing. (You will use a little over 1 cup of the dye solution.)

10. With the tablespoon, carefully spoon the highlight color onto the wool in the blank spaces. Do not blend; let the colors stand on their own. You will see blank spaces between the three colors.

11. Pour ½ cup of vinegar over the entire pan of wool.

12. Let the wool simmer (not boil) for 25 to 30 minutes or until the water under the dyed wool is clear. Do not let the water evaporate from the pan or you will burn your wool.

13. Remove the spot dyed wool from the pot into a separate clean pan. A good pan to use is a square enamel or stainless-steel pan.

14. Rinse the wool in cool water and line dry, or dry in a dryer on the lowest setting.

Some Spot Dye Color Combinations We Love
(using W. Cushing & Co. Acid Dyes)

Main Color: Bronze Green
Second Color: Aqua
Highlight Color: Mint Green

Main Color: Bright Purple
Second Color: Lavender
Highlight Color: Aqualon Wine

Main Color: Rust
Second Color: Apricot
Highlight Color: Buttercup Yellow

Main Color: Golden Brown
Second Color: Peach
Highlight Color: Turkey Red

Main Color: Bronze Green
Second Color: Aqua
Highlight Color: Mint Green

Main Color: Navy Blue
Second Color: Copenhagen Blue
Highlight Color: Aqualon Blue

Main Color: Crimson
Second Color: Redgrape
Highlight Color: Pink

Casserole Spot Dyeing

Casserole spot dyeing is one of the favorite dyeing methods among those rug hookers who have bits or pieces of wool or use "as is" wool, such as clothing. It is different from spot dyeing because it uses a small pan and small amounts of wool, which are tailored to their intended purpose.

It is a thrifty way to dye, and the small amounts of wool that are left over after you have hooked your project are always useful for small touches in other projects. They never go to waste.

All the colors for a given casserole are "cooked" in the same pan, at the same time, yet they retain their own identity; greens stay green, golds stay gold, blues stay blue. Where the colors meet, beautiful and unusual hues are created. These are the happy accidents of unlimited hues, tints, values, and shades.

How do we do it? Simple. The individual dyes are spooned onto wet wools that are laid flat in a pan with the same dimensions (or slightly larger) than the wool pieces.

It is very important to match the size of the wool pieces to the pan size. Doing so keeps water from flowing freely around the wool, which would mix up the dyes too much. We use as little water as possible—just enough to keep the wool moist while it is "cooking" in the oven.

It is a good idea to collect a few different sizes of enamel or stainless-steel pans. One of the most popular sizes measures about 8" x 6" x 2" deep. To prepare, tear the wool the same size as the pan or slightly smaller. If you have some wool pieces already torn that you want to use and they are smaller, just lay them side by side to fill the space at the bottom of your pan.

Don't limit yourself to only white wool. This casserole spot dyeing method lets you use colored wools, too. If you use different colored wools, put the darkest wools in the pan first, and progress up through the medium and light-colored wools, with the white or lightest-colored wool at the top.

By using strong dye solutions on the dark wool in the bottom of the pan, then diluting those dye solutions with a little plain water to use on the medium and light-colored wools, you will get a great variety of colors in one pan.

Tip!

Separate Layers with Paper Towels

More than one piece of wool can be dyed in the pan at the same time. By layering white paper towels between the wool pieces, you can achieve radical changes of color. The paper towels will soak up excess dye, preventing it from entering a piece of wool that you do not wish to dye. Do not use colored towels, or you may get some colors in your wools you were not expecting!

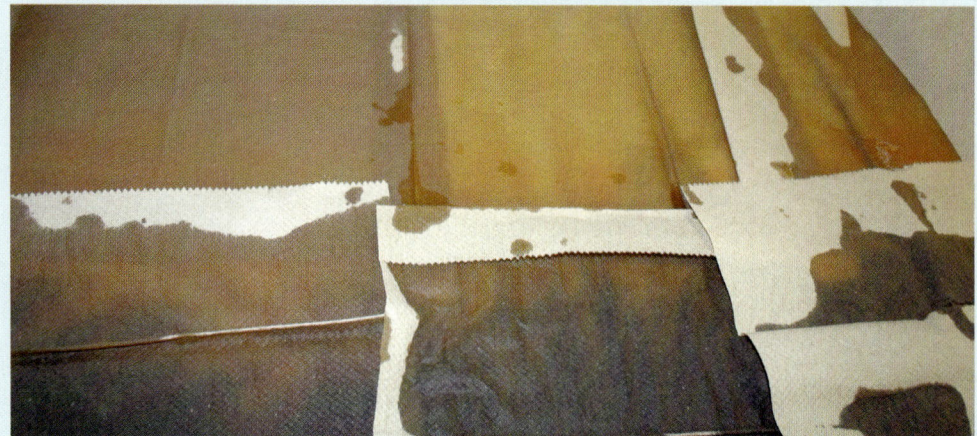

The bottom layer of wool placed in the casserole pan

First dye added to the bottom layer

Second dye added to the bottom layer

Third dye added to the bottom layer

Second layer of wool with dye added

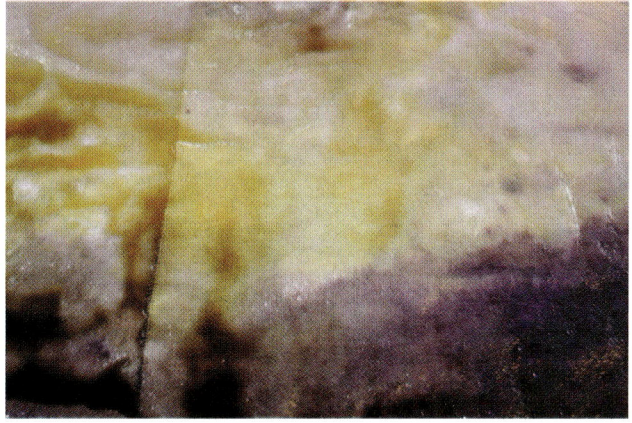

Third (top) layer of wool with dye added

Finished wool from the bottom layer. Note the deep, intense colors.

Finished wool from the middle layer. These colors are more mid-tone.

Finished wool from the top layer. These are the lightest, most pastel colors.

"Spotty" Spot Dyeing Method – What You Need

- Wool: 1 yard plus 2", wet and soaked in warm water with Lemon Joy
- Acid dyes
- Enamel or stainless-steel flat pan, 16" x 24" or smaller
- Dye spoons: ¼ tsp. and ½ tsp.
- Three 2-cup glass measuring cups
- Metal tablespoon
- Citric acid or white vinegar
- Heat source of your choice
- Wooden spoon
- Rectangular pan
- Electric kettle

PREPARING THE DYE SOLUTION & PLACEMENT OF DYES

Measure ½ tsp. acid dye into a measuring cup; add 1 cup boiling water and stir thoroughly until dye is dissolved. You will spoon the dye onto the wool; never pour the dye or too much liquid will collect in the bottom of the pan.

Usually three or four dyes are applied on a single piece of wool. It is easy to lose track of what you are doing and get them mixed up, so get into the habit of keeping them in order. The best way to keep them in order is to go from dark to light or light to dark.

Usually you will use three colors: the base color, the secondary color or colors, and the highlight or lightest color. By correctly combining the three colors, you will have a dyed piece of wool that has depth, highlights, and shading—all in one piece.

For this dye method, you will not use all your dye in the bottom layer; you can continue by layering up to the top of the pan.

The main color is the color that you wish to see the most, and it should be the darkest of the three colors. It sets the tone for the entire piece. For example, if you are casserole dyeing for a daffodil, you might start with Old Gold.

Your secondary color or colors should blend with your main color; it should be a strong color to stand up to your main color, but not overpower it. The secondary color is sometimes the hardest color to choose: remember, less intense is better. The secondary color should be one that you like as it will appear almost as often as the main color. Two colors that blend with Old Gold and are strong enough to stand up to Old Gold are Buttercup or Gold.

The highlight color, chosen to highlight both your main color and secondary color, should be the lightest of the three colors. Think of a color that will add light to the other two colors. In our daffodil example, the highlight color might be Lemon.

As you gain experience in casserole spot dyeing, you will be able to look at the motif you are dyeing for (a flower, leaf, fruit, tree, animal, bird, or whatever), decide what colors you need, what proportion, and where they are in relation to each other. The dyes are simply spooned onto the wool, close to each other, or overlapping slightly, depending on what you need for your piece.

STEP-BY-STEP CASSEROLE SPOT DYE INSTRUCTIONS

1. How to apply the dyes: The dyes (as specified in the color combination box on page 47) are spooned on. They need to be blended into the wool by rubbing them in a zigzag motion with the back of a spoon.

2. Layer the wool, separated by paper if you wish. Add dye to each layer as described in step 1.

3. Apply vinegar: Sprinkle about a tablespoon of vinegar over the pan as evenly as you can. This vinegar goes onto every piece of dyed wool. Sometimes, when dyeing a lot of pieces, as they pile up with dye solution and vinegar, you may begin to get too much liquid. If this occurs, just tip the pan and carefully pour off the excess liquid. You only need about ¼" of liquid in the pan.

4. How to set the dyes: Cover the pan tightly with aluminum foil or a lid. We can simmer our casserole on the top of the stove if we wish, about 30 to 45 minutes. Be sure to check that there is enough liquid in the pan to keep the wool from burning. If necessary, add more plain hot water during the cooking phase, making sure that it penetrates to the bottom layer of the wool. You don't want it to boil dry. A safe method is to put it into the oven at about 300 degrees for about one hour.

5. Rinse the wools thoroughly, then dry the wool.

Tip!

Sometimes (often!) it is easy to forget what we did. If you got a particularly beautiful piece of wool, or if you think you may need more of a color, you have to remember so that you can reproduce it. Make notes in your notebook as you go. You will be glad that you did!

Spot dyed wool combines nicely with textures to add depth, definition, and direction to your rug hooking.

Dye Method: Abrash (Hunter Green, Orange, Old Gold)

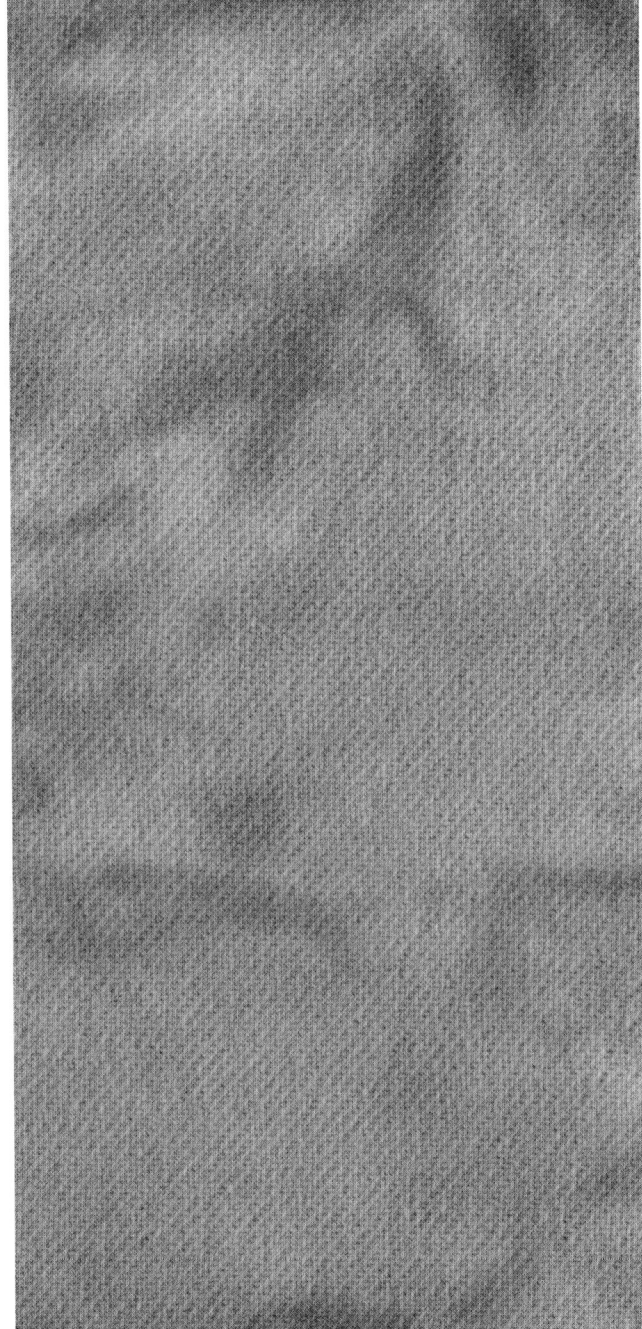

Dye Method: Beautifully Blended Spot Dye
(Silver Gray, Pink, and Purple)

Casserole Spot Dye Color Combinations
(using W. Cushing & Co. Acid Dyes)

Main Color: Crimson
Second Color: Cherry
Highlight Color: Rose

Main Color: Coral
Second Color: Peach
Highlight Color: Salmon

Main Color: Bright Purple
Second Color: Apricot
Highlight Color: Buttercup Yellow

Main Color: Salmon
Second Color: Peach
Highlight Color: Rose Pink

Main Color: Canary
Second Color: Aqualon Yellow
Highlight Color: Ecru

Main Color: Khaki
Second Color: Olive Green
Highlight Color: Bronze

Main Color: Seal Brown
Second Color: Medium Brown
Highlight Color: Taupe

Diving into the Dye Pot

Swatch Dyeing (No Jars Required!)

The variation of values of one color

Notice the different values you can get with this swatch dyeing method

Many rug hookers love to use wool that is dyed in swatches. Swatches are graduated shades of one color in separate pieces, not in one piece of wool like a dip dye. Swatches come in 4, 6, or 8 separate pieces of wool, ranging from dark to light values of that color.

Swatch-dyed wool is a traditional method of dyeing and normally would use 4 to 8 jars to dye the wool. For this reason, many rug hookers shy away from swatch dyeing. They do not want to have to keep the jars, if storage is an issue, and some dyers want to dye larger pieces of wool.

However, there is another method that does not involve jars but will give you 4, 6, or 8 swatches. You just have to have a timer or watch by your side!

Start with a dye bath of the color you would like. You have to make this dye bath stronger than normal because you will be getting 4 to 8 shades from it. So what constitutes a strong dye bath? Instead of using ¼ teaspoon of dry dye in 4 cups of boiling water, you will use 1 to 2 teaspoons of dry dye in 4 cups of boiling water.

For making swatches with this method, cut the wool in fat quarters (18" x 36"). You will end up with a quarter yard of each shade. If you don't need a quarter yard, cut the wool to 9" x 18" (an ⅛ yard). Cut as many pieces of wool for as many shades as you would like (usually 4, 6, or 8).

Pre-soak your wool well so that it will grab the dye as soon as it is put in the dye bath. Since we want the dye to grab quickly, the vinegar or citric acid will be added directly to the dye bath. This is added insurance so you can get all the shades you want.

How would you use swatches? Any way you want. You will have all shades of one color for sky, water, flowers, scrolls, and animals.

SWATCH DYEING METHOD – WHAT YOU NEED

- Wool: 1-2 yards, depending on how many values you want, cut into 8" x 36" or 9" x 18" pieces, pre-soaked in warm water and a small amount of Lemon Joy.

- Acid dye

- Enamel or stainless-steel pot: 4-quart or larger

- Dye spoon: 1 tsp.

- One 4-cup glass measuring cup

- Metal tablespoon

- Citric acid or white vinegar

- Heat source of your choice

- Wooden spoon

- Rectangular pan

- Electric kettle

STEP-BY-STEP SWATCH DYEING INSTRUCTIONS

1. Pre-soak your wool in warm water and use a little Lemon Joy to open up the fibers. Soak the wool for a few hours or overnight. Be sure your wool is thoroughly soaked so the dye will grab the wool.

2. Let the wool drain in the sink. Do not squeeze out excess water.

3. Fill a 4-quart or larger pot half full and bring to a simmer (no bubbles, just steam).

4. Prepare the dye solution: Mix 1 tsp. of acid dye into a glass measuring cup and add 4 cups boiling water. If the color is too light, add 1 more tsp. of dye. Stir well: every granule of dye must be dissolved before proceeding.

5. Pour the dye solution into the simmering pot of water. This is your dye bath.

6. Take your first piece of wet wool and, without wringing it out, drop it into the dye bath. Set your timer for 8 minutes. Make sure the piece of wool is covered and absorbing the dye. Stir it a few times.

7. After 8 minutes, take your next piece of wet wool and drop it into the dye bath. Reset the timer to 7 minutes. Make sure both pieces of wool are covered and in the dye bath. Stir a few times with a wooden spoon.

8. After 7 minutes, take your next piece of wet wool and drop it into the dye bath. Reset the timer to 6 minutes. Make sure all the wool is covered and in the dye bath. Stir with a wooden spoon.

9. After 6 minutes, take your next piece of wet wool and drop it into the dye bath. Reset the timer for 5 minutes. Make sure all the wool is covered and in the dye bath. Stir with a wooden spoon.

10. After 5 minutes, take your next piece of wet wool and drop it into the dye bath. Reset the timer for 5 minutes. Make sure all the wool is covered and in the dye bath. Stir with a wooden spoon.

11. Continue in this fashion until all your wool is in the dye bath or your dye bath is clear.

12. Remove all the pieces of wool and place them in a flat pan to cool. Do not let the individual pieces of wool touch or lay on top of each other. Each one should be separate. Use two pans if necessary.

13. Rinse the wool in cool, not cold, water. Cold water might shock the wool and cause it to felt. Line dry or dry in a dryer on the lowest setting.

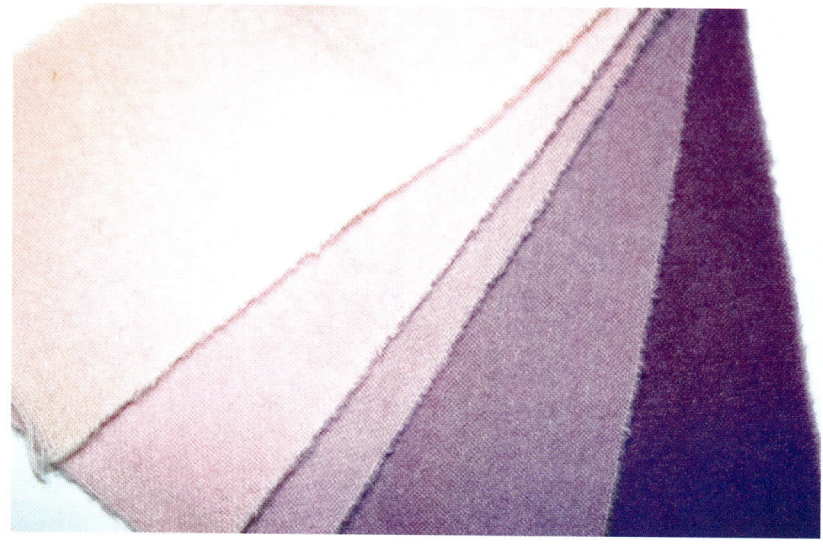

Dye Method: Spot Dye (Sangria)

Dye Method: Spot Dye (Fall Pumpkin Patch)

Snow/Ice Dyeing

We all know that a good fresh snow is great to clean our hooked rugs. Did you also know that it can be used to dye unique one-of-a kind wool for your rugs? Dyeing wool with snow is not an exact science. It is a way to enjoy a snowstorm without bundling up. While a wet, heavy snow is not good for our power lines, it is good for dyeing—fluffy dry snow does not work as well.

Your color combinations are endless when you snow dye. This is a great project to do with your friends to beat those winter blues.

Snow and Ice Dyeing - What You Need

- Wool: 1 yd., wet and soaked in warm water with Lemon Joy.
- Acid Dyes
- Enamel or stainless-steel flat pan
- Dye spoons
- 2-cup glass measuring cup: one for each dye color
- Citric acid or white vinegar
- Wooden spoon
- White paper towels
- Rectangular pan
- Aluminum foil
- Snow or ice

Step-by-Step Snow/Ice Dyeing Instructions: Method One

1. Pre-soak your wool in warm water and use a little Lemon Joy to open up the fibers. You can soak your wool for a few hours or overnight (even before the first flake falls).

2. Scrunch your wool like you would for a spot dye. The amount of wool you use is based on your pan or turkey roaster. "Crowd" the pan. By crowding the pan you allow the colors to flow and mix, creating unique combinations of colors.

3. Pack the fresh snow (or ice) in a firm layer on top of the wool. Be sure that all the wool is covered and there is a good layer of snow over the wool.

Tip!

You can use different wools such as solids in white, cream, pink, and yellow and textures to get more colors that can mix for backgrounds.

4. Make your dye solution. (Find several recipes in Chapter 10). Pour your dye solution or dye recipe over the snow or ice. When you are done, the snow looks like a slushy or an Italian ice.

5. Place aluminum foil over the pan and turn your burners on to medium heat. Cook for 20 minutes. Check after 10 minutes to ensure that you have enough water in the pan. Do not stir.

6. After 20 minutes, pour ½ cup of vinegar over the wool. Any wool not covered in dye should be moved around so it is covered with dye solution.

7. Cover the pan again and cook an additional 10 minutes on medium heat. Be sure you have enough water in the pan.

8. Turn off the heat; let the wool cool for 10 to 15 minutes. Remove the aluminum foil.

9. Gently rinse your wool and dry as normal.

Diving into the Dye Pot | 53

Step-by-Step Snow/Ice Dyeing Instructions: Method Two

1. Pre-soak your wool in warm water and use a little Lemon Joy to open up the fibers. Soak your wool for a few hours or overnight.

2. Scrunch your wool like you would for a spot dye. The amount of wool you use is based on the size of your pan or turkey roaster. Crowd the pan.

3. Pack the fresh snow in a firm layer on top of the wool. Be sure that all the wool is covered and there is a good layer of snow over the wool. This is very important.

4. Sprinkle dry dye over the ice in any design you like. Be careful not to over-sprinkle the dye as it may not absorb fully. If the dye does not fully absorb, your water will never be clear. For our example, we sprinkled W. Cushing's Aqualon Blue, Baby Blue, Light Blue, Copenhagen Blue, and Blue.

5. Place aluminum foil over the pan and turn your burners on to medium heat for 20 minutes. Check after 10 minutes to be sure you have enough water in the pan, but do not stir.

6. After 20 minutes, pour ½ cup vinegar over the wool. Any wool not covered in liquid should be moved around so it is covered with dye solution.

7. Cover the pan again and cook an additional 10 minutes on medium heat. Be sure there is enough water in your pan.

8. Turn off the heat, and let the wool cool for 10 to 15 minutes.

9. Gently rinse your wool and dry as normal.

Hint!

You can use different colors of wool to get more colors that you can mix for backgrounds. When sprinkling the dry dye onto the wool, treat it like salt on food: less is more!

Clean a Wool Rug with Snow

On a cold, clear day (25°F or colder), with at least several inches of fresh powder (not wet, heavy snow), take your wool rug outside and lay it on fresh snow, face down.

Gently push fresh powdery snow onto the rug and let the rug sit for 15-20 minutes. Your rug will become stiff. Then gently shake the rug out. You can beat the exposed surface with a soft broom.

Turn the rug over on the right side onto a clean patch of snow and repeat.

Brush off all visible snow. Leave it outside, preferably hanging over a railing (as long as it is not snowing or raining), another hour or so to let sublimation (the cold-weather process whereby snow or ice transforms directly from solid to vapor) do its work. The rug should then be clean and dry.

Don't return the rug to its place inside until it is completely dry.

By putting the rug over a railing or chair, you are allowing the cold air to flow around the rug. An average size rug takes 28 to 30 hours to dry in good weather conditions outside or inside your garage or basement. Be aware, your rug could take up to 36 to 40 hours to dry.

Yarn Dyeing

Dyeing wool yarn for rug hooking, rug punching, and whipping is similar to dyeing wool fabric. When using 100% wool yarn, acid dyes work best and give you a true color, right to the center of the yarn.

Your yarn can be any weight you choose, from sport weight (which is a lightweight wool) to bulky. For those who have knit or crocheted and built up a stash of yarns, this is a productive way to repurpose those leftover skeins.

(Please note: if your yarn is 100% cotton, use W. Cushing & Co.'s Direct Dye, designed for cotton or synthetic fabrics.)

When dyeing wool yarn, the basic principles are the same as dyeing wool fabric. For a wonderful finished edge to your rug, dye your yarn the same as your background color wool yardage.

Wool yarn does need to soak in warm water for a few hours or overnight. Do not use boiling water or you will felt the yarn. Overnight soaking seems to work best to avoid having the center of the yarn not dye properly (which shows when you whip with the yarn). The tighter spun and thicker the yarn, the longer you will need to soak it to make sure the dye absorbs to the center.

You can always add dye during the dyeing process; just remember, you can't subtract it. So be sure to start with a lighter dye solution and then add to it if you need to.

Some people add dye powder directly to the dye bath. We recommend mixing 1-2 tsps. of dye in two cups of boiling water, and then adding portions of this solution to your dye bath. This dye solution will stay fresh for several months in a jar with a tight lid.

If you decide to add dye during the process, remove the yarn and return it to the bath once you have added dye and it is completely mixed in. (Adding dye when your material is in the dye bath might result in spots and variations.)

Just like with wool, using gray, camel, or beige yarns will give you a varied look and wonderful rich dyed colors. Any dye recipe you use and like for wool fabric, including spot dyeing, can be used for yarn.

Yarn Dyeing – What You Need

- Wool yarn in a skein: ¼ lb. or 4 oz. or 100 grams, presoaked in warm water with Lemon Joy
- Acid dyes
- Enamel or stainless-steel 1- or 2-qt. pot
- Dye spoon: ¼ tsp.
- 4-cup glass measuring cup
- White vinegar
- Heat source
- Wooden spoon
- Tongs
- Rectangular pan

Step-by-Step Yarn Dyeing Instructions

1. Prepare the yarn. Your yarn should be clean. Unwrap the skein into a loose loop and tie in several places around the skein without cinching so it doesn't tangle.

2. Soak the skein for few a hours in warm water with a few drops of Lemon Joy. This "wetting" prepares the yarn to take up the dye. You cannot soak too long; we recommend overnight. Drain the wool but do not let it dry.

3. Prepare your dye bath. Put enough water in your pot so that your yarn will be completely covered, and can be stirred. About a gallon of water will work for one skein of yarn. Add about ¼ cup of vinegar for one skein (but more vinegar does no harm, and can help overcome difficulties caused by variations in your water chemistry).

4. Add 1-2 tsps. dye to 4 cups boiling water. This is your dye solution.

5. Pour the dye solution into your dye bath.

6. Add your wet yarn and begin to heat. You want the water to simmer, but not to come to a full boil. Gently stir your bath regularly as it heats and simmers. You will notice that the dye bath will become clearer and clearer as the dye solution is taken up into yarn.

7. If the yarn is removed from the dye bath prematurely, you may get uneven or off-shade dyeing. It is important to let the material simmer for a good while, 30-40 minutes or until you have the shade you want and your water is mostly clear. You cannot rush this process.

8. After the dye bath has exhausted (the water is clear in the pot), remove the dye pot from the heat and allow it to return to room temperature. Rinse the material with cold water and let dry. Do not pour hot water over your yarn or change the temperature of your wash or rinse bath too drastically; you may felt your yarn.

9. Let the yarn air dry.

Dyeing Yarn with Wool—In the Same Pot!

Dye wool yardage and wool yarn in the same pot to create matching wool fabric and wool yarn. The two pieces will be harmonious and will make a wonderful enhancement to your rug hooking or punching.

It is best to pick one of the dye formulas when dyeing fabric and yarn together—any dye recipe you use and like for wool fabric, including spot dyeing, can be used.

You must double the dye solutions—one for the yarn and one for the wool—so that both pieces absorb the same amount of dye. Just as when you dye wool fabric, using gray, camel, or beige yarns will give you a varied look and wonderful richly dyed colors.

This is what you need:
- Wool yarn in a skein, ¼ lb./4 oz./100 grams, wet and soaked
- Half a yard of wool fabric, wet and soaked
- Acid dyes in the colors of your recipe
- Enamel or stainless-steel rectangular pan, like a lasagna pan
- Dye spoon: ¼ tsp.
- Two 4-cup glass measuring cups, one for the yarn and one for the wool fabric
- White vinegar
- Heat source
- Wooden spoon
- Tongs

Directions for dyeing:

1. Prepare the yarn. Be sure that it is clean.

2. Unwrap the skein into a loose loop; tie loosely in several places around the skein (without cinching) so the yarn won't tangle.

3. Soak the skein for a few hours in warm water with a few drops of Lemon Joy. This wetting process prepares the yarn to take up the dye. You cannot soak too long; we recommend soaking overnight. Drain the wool but do not let it dry.

4. Soak the wool fabric just as you would for any dye recipe.

5. Prepare the dye solution. Mix up the dye recipe twice into 4 cups boiling water. One is for the yarn and one is for the wool. This is the dye solution.

6. Prepare the pan.

    a. Place the yarn in half of the rectangular pan. Be careful not to tangle or overlap.

    b. Place the wool in the other half of the pan. Be careful to not overlap or touch the yarn.

7. Pour one 4-cup measure of dye solution over the yarn. Some of the dye solution may run to the wool—that is just fine. Make sure the yarn is covered in the dye solution and the entire skein is covered, no white spots.

8. Pour the second 4-cup measure over the wool. Make sure the wool is completely covered. Some of the dye solution may run back to the yarn, and that is fine. Make sure the wool is completely covered, no white spots.

9. Mix ¼ cup vinegar with ¼ cup water. Pour over both the wool and yarn.

10. Set the heat to medium and let the pan cook on the stove top for 20 minutes, or until the dye bath has exhausted.

11. Remove the pan from the heat and allow the materials to return to room temperature. Rinse the yarn with cold water and let it dry. Do not pour hot water over your yarn or change the temperature of your wash or rinse bath too drastically—that may felt the yarn. Rinse the wool as normal.

12. Let the yarn air dry; dry the wool as you normally would.

Dyeing Antique Black

Antique black is a black that has been worn, mottled, and has a shine due to age and use. It is a popular color for backgrounds, especially when hooking an antique rug pattern.

The most important thing to remember when dyeing antique black is that it is not just one color. Antique black is a mixture of many colors, combined to give the look and feel of old, aged black. It adds movement and dimension.

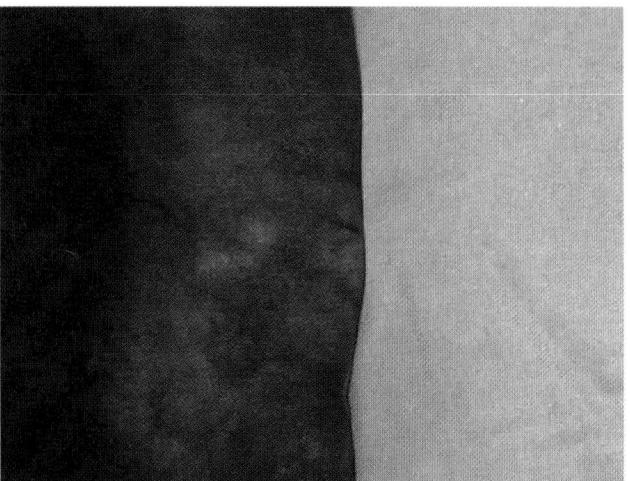

Step-by-Step Dyeing Antique Black Instructions: Method One – Over Solid Wools

1. Gather solid colored wools together (wools such as red, blue, green, purple, maroon, and bright yellow). Use any combination that amounts to 1 to 1½ yards.

2. Soak overnight in warm water and Lemon Joy.

3. Bring a pot of water with enough water to cover all the wool to a simmer (no bubbles).

4. Make three dye solutions:

    a. 4 cups boiling water plus ¼ tsp. Dark Green

    b. 4 cups boiling water plus ⅛ tsp. Burgundy

    c. 4 cups boiling water plus 1/32 tsp. Peacock

5. Pour each dye solution into the pot of simmering water. This is the dye bath.

6. Add all your wools and stir vigorously so that all the wools are immersed.

7. After 20 minutes, add ¼ cup vinegar and let simmer for another 8-10 minutes.

8. Turn off the heat and let it sit for at least one hour. You can let it sit overnight.

9. Rinse the wool in cool water and dry.

Step-by-Step Dyeing Antique Black Instructions:
Method Two – Dyeing Over Your Leftovers

1. Gather all of your harshly colored wools together including checks and plaids that are brightly colored. The total amount of wool should be 1–1½ yards.

2. Soak overnight in warm water and Lemon Joy.

3. Bring a pot of water with enough water to cover all the wool to a simmer (no bubbles).

4. Make 5 dye solutions, each in 4 cups boiling water.

    a. 4 cups boiling water plus ¼ tsp. Turquoise

    b. 4 cups boiling water plus ⅛ tsp. Hunter Green

    c. 4 cups boiling water plus ⅛ tsp. Burgundy

    d. 4 cups boiling water plus ¹⁄₃₂ tsp. Peacock

    e. 4 cups boiling water plus ¹⁄₃₂ tsp. of Redgrape

5. Pour each dye solution into the pot of simmering water. This is the dye bath.

6. Add all your wools and stir vigorously so that all the wools are immersed.

7. After 20 minutes, add ¼ cup of vinegar and let simmer for another 8 to 10 minutes.

8. Turn off the heat and let sit it for at least one hour. You can let it sit overnight.

9. Rinse in cool water and dry.

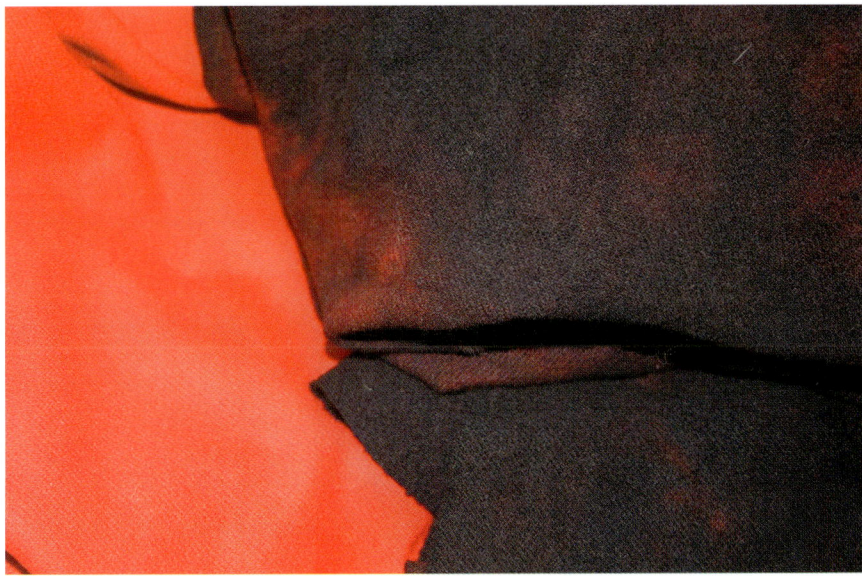

6 — Alternative Methods of Dyeing Wool

Can you dye without acid dyes? Can you dye without a dye kitchen? Yes, you can!

Sometimes it is not possible to have a dye kitchen and some people simply do not want to have to store acid dyes and all the equipment. Many fiber artists have large stashes, whether the wool be in yardage or wool clothing collected over the years. The colors of the wool in stashes may be what they previously wanted, but our color taste changes over the years. What can we do with these "old" colors? Luckily, wool is still wool; the question is this: how can we make it useful?

Luckily, there are ways. These alternative methods of dyeing wool allow you to change the colors in your stash—with your stash!

The wool you will dye from these methods will be unique and one of a kind. While the process of dyeing wool this way is easy and rewarding, it is often truly one of a kind and not to be repeated. It can be difficult to repeat to get the same color later.

Why? Because you are using the existing dye in your wool and transferring to other wools. The transfer process is the same but the amount of different dyes in the wool changes from piece to piece.

The dyed wool using these methods will be muted (but not necessarily dull) and have a vintage, soft appearance. These wools are great for hooking many things: flowers of all colors; skies, mountains, and water for pictorials; accents for Orientals; calm backgrounds or subtle outlines for geometrics.

Or consider scrolls. While dip-dyed wools create the scroll, the center of the scroll normally needs to have a soft or speckled effect to create movement. The wools dyed using any of the methods in this chapter are perfect.

Tip!

As you hook with this wool, combine it with striped textures and pot-dyed wools. These wools will act as highlights. For example, you are hooking grapes and are using your dip-dyed wool for the grapes. The highlight that is crucial in a grape to make it round and appear to be in a bunch of grapes comes from the textures.

DYEING WOOL WITH CLOTHING LININGS AND TIDE

This easy going method of dyeing gives you a marbleized, soft look and takes the harshness out of solid colored wools. I have done this to make bright red appear soft and vintage. This method of dyeing works for those with a busy schedule as you do not have to be specific with measurements or watch the dye pot continually. Once you turn off your heat source, you can let the wool sit in the water for up to 6 hours. The end result is beautifully dyed wool.

Dyeing your wool without acid dyes is not hard. If you have been avoiding the dye pot, this method allows you to experience the wonder of dyeing before making the investment into all the dyeing equipment.

In this method, you are using linings from clothing and Tide instead of acid dyes. We use the linings as the source of the dye. Yes, they may be silk or acrylic, but they work wonderfully in this dye process.

This works because you have two distinct types of fabric in the dye pot: bleeders and blondes. The bleeders are the source of the dye: they "bleed" the color onto the blondes, which are the receivers of the dye.

The disadvantage of this approach is that if you get a color you like, it is hard to repeat it. The bleeders may work for one or two dye pots but not much more, and you cannot wrap the wool exactly the same each time, so the effect will be different.

Hints!

- A tall dye pot works well for this method of dyeing. Be sure the wool is covered with simmering water.

- You can use an enamel roasting pan with a lid for this method of dyeing.

- Vibrant clothing linings bleed best.

- Neutral colored acrylic liners like beige or brown work best on white or natural colored wool. These liners give the wool an aged look.

Fabric Types

The Bleeders: (the colors of linings that work best to give the dye): green, red, orange, burgundy, purple, orange, teal, gold. (Remember: the darker the better, as the color will "bleed" or "run" from the liner.)

The Blondes: (the colors of wools that receive the dye best): white, ecru, off-white, yellow, pink, baby blue, sage green, lilac, gray, tangerine, etc. The wool does not have to be solid—herringbones, light plaids (with lots of white), and light tweeds work as well. (Remember: the lighter the better.)

The linings can be used several times.

Step-by-Step Instructions

1. Cut your wool no wider than 9" and no longer than 36" to make it easy to layer and roll. All your wool does not have to be cut exactly the same size.

2. Soak the wool for about 30 minutes prior to dyeing. Be sure to add Lemon Joy to open up the fibers.

3. Fill the dye pot to about 4" from the top and bring the water to a simmer.

4. Add 2 to 3 Tbsp. of Tide. (Use the Tide without bleach.)

5. Layer the wool with the acrylic linings from skirts, suits, and pants. The brighter the colors, the better.

6. Tightly roll the wool lengthwise, with linings in between. Twist the bundle like a snake and tie it with string to hold everything in place.

7. Put the rolls in the simmering water and cover. Simmer for 15 minutes.

8. Now add ½ cup vinegar to the water and let it cook for an additional 10–15 minutes.

9. Peek to see if you like the color. If you do, remove the rolls and rinse thoroughly in cool water. If they don't seem "done," let the rolls soak another 5 minutes maximum, then remove and rinse thoroughly. You can let the rolls soak overnight if you wish.

10. After the wool is rinsed, dry as you normally would.

Marbleizing Wool with Recycled and As-Is Solid Colored Wools

This method of dyeing gives you a marbleized, soft look and takes harshness out of solid colored wools. It is a great way to recycle wools, such as skirts, jackets, or even new solid-color yardage.

STEP-BY-STEP INSTRUCTIONS

1. Prepare the wool to dye. Cut the wool no wider than 9" and no longer than 36" to make it easier to layer and roll. All your wool does not have to be cut into the exactly same size.

2. Soak the wool for about 30 minutes prior to dyeing. Add some Lemon Joy to open up the fibers.

3. Fill the dye pot to about 4" from the top and bring the water to a simmer.

4. Add 1 Tbsp. of Jet Dry and 2 to 3 Tbsp. of Tide; use the Tide without bleach.

5. Layer your bleeding wool alternately with the white or blond wool. The brighter the colors of bleeders, the better.

6. Tightly roll the wool lengthwise. Twist the bundle like a snake and tie with string to hold everything in place.

7. Put the rolls in the simmering water. Cover the dye pot and simmer for 10 minutes.

8. Add ½ cup vinegar to the water and let cook for an additional 10–12 minutes.

9. Peek to see if you like the color. If you do, remove the rolls and rinse thoroughly in cool water. If it does not look "done," let the rolls soak another 3 minutes maximum, then remove and rinse thoroughly. It is very easy to burn your wool if you do not keep an eye on the dye pot.

10. Dry as you would normally. The bleeding wool will be lighter in color and okay to use as is, or to use again in another dye batch.

1. Colorful wools used in marbleizing technique

5. Place the wools on the base white or blond wool

6. Wools rolled together

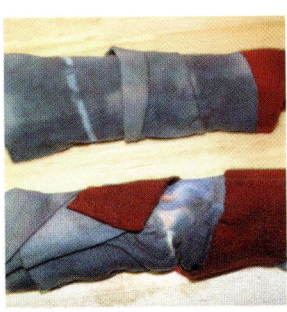 

9. Wet rolls from the dye pot *9. Wet rolls from the dye pot, unrolled*

Alternative Methods of Dyeing Wool | 65

Removing Color from Wool

Cook Method

Do you have a piece of wool that is just too intense, too bright? Removing color from wool is fun, fascinating, and full of surprises. With this process, you control how much color you want to remove; how much wool to use; and it does not matter if the wool is textured, "as is," dyed, or solid.

There is a lot of satisfaction when you are able to use wools in your stash you otherwise have deemed useless. The results are surprising and sometimes more beautiful than any planned dye pot.

COOK METHOD – WHAT YOU NEED

- Wool
- Enamel or stainless-steel 4- or 6-qt. pot
- Tablespoon
- Tongs
- Ammonia
- White vinegar
- Heat source
- Rectangular pan

STEP-BY-STEP COOK METHOD INSTRUCTIONS

1. Tear your wool (all of the same color) into quarter or half yard pieces, depending on the size of your pot.

2. Fill a 4-qt. pot two thirds full of water and add 2–3 tablespoons of ammonia.

3. Add wool pieces, but do not create a crowded pot.

4. Bring the pot to a simmer, do not boil. Boiling could damage the wool. Simmer for one minute to 20 minutes; the length of time depends on the original color of the wool, the quality of the wool, and the depth of color desired.

5. When enough color is removed, rinse the wool several times in warm water.

6. In a clean pot, simmer fresh water and add 3 Tbsp. white vinegar to the water and wool pieces. Simmer for 15 minutes.

7. Rinse and dry wool.

Non-Cook Method

While this process takes more time, it is simple and does a large quantity of wool at once.

Non-Cook Method – What You Need

- Wool
- Large sink or pan or tub
- Tongs or wooden spoon
- Ammonia
- Rubber gloves
- White vinegar

Step-by-Step Non-Cook Method Instructions

1. Fill a large sink, pan, or tub with enough hot water to cover the wool you wish to remove the color from.

2. Add to this water ¼ cup of ammonia. Be sure to work in a well-ventilated room. Stir with a wooden spoon or tongs.

3. Add the wool. Push it down into the water to make sure all the wool has contact with the water.

4. Let the wool soak in the solution for 8 to 12 hours. Remember, you do not put this over heat.

5. After 8 to 12 hours, rinse the wool thoroughly to remove all the remaining color. It is best to wear rubber gloves.

6. To set the remaining color, refill the sink, pan, or tub with hot water and add ¼ cup white vinegar. Let the wool soak for 10–15 minutes; rinse and dry.

7 — Easy Techniques for Unique Effects

Uncertain about which dye method you want to start with? Want to have fun in the dye pot with your fellow fiber artists?

I've listed a few methods here for you to try out as you explore dyeing. The wools created will be unique and hard to duplicate; however, you will have fun, learn a lot, and create beautiful dyed wool for your stash.

DUMP-AND-GO DYEING

Dye Method: Dump and Go (Copenhagen Blue, Navy Blue, Rust, Silver Gray)

This quick and easy method of dyeing works well for dyeing large quantities of wool. Perhaps you need a background: consider this dye method to achieve a varied background instead of using many textures or colors.

The dump-and-go method is like a potluck supper—everyone brings something, and you never know what to expect. Even though you do not know what is coming, the result is always great!

STEP-BY-STEP DUMP-AND-GO DYEING INSTRUCTIONS

1. Pre-soak your wool in warm water; use a little Lemon Joy to open up the fibers. Soak it for a few hours or overnight.

2. The size of the dye pot depends on the amount of wool you plan to dye. A 6-quart pot is handy; you can use your turkey roaster as a pot.

3. Fill your pot three fourths of the way to the top.

4. Heat to steaming, not to a full boil.

5. Mix the dye colors in a 2-cup glass measuring cup. Add ¼ tsp. citric acid to each measuring cup.

6. Mix up 2 to 5 different dyes, in separate measuring cups. You are only limited by how many measuring cups you have!

7. Put the soaked wool in the pot; make sure the water covers the wool. Add more boiling water if needed.

8. Dump the first dye color into the pot; stir once or twice with a wooden spoon.

9. Repeat step 8 with the remaining colors, stirring once or twice after each addition.

10. Let simmer for 20–28 minutes, until the dye bath is almost clear.

11. Turn off the heat and let the pot sit overnight.

12. Next day, remove your wool from the pot into a clean pan.

13. Rinse your wool in cool water and line dry or dry in a dryer on the lowest setting.

Hints!

- For fun, pick colors you do not normally use. This is a great way to expand your color palette.

- Don't use more than ¾ yd. of wool in an electric turkey roaster.

- If you are dyeing with a group of friends, have each person select a color.

- You must let the dye pot sit overnight to get the maximum effect.

- If you get wool that did not mottle, you may have put too much wool into the pot.

Dry Dyeing—The Lasagna Method

Dry dyed wool ready to be hooked! Colors used: green, yellow, bright purple and magenta

Dry dyeing simply means that we sprinkle dry dye powders onto wet wool, and then we steam the wool to set the dyes. The specks of dyes stay exactly where they landed because we add salt to the dry dye. The color stays on the spot where it lands and is not diffused as in regular "wet" dyeing.

We add salt to the dry dye before sprinkling, and mix it thoroughly. The salt does two things. It separates the dye particles, making it easy to distribute them fairly evenly, and it sets the dyes.

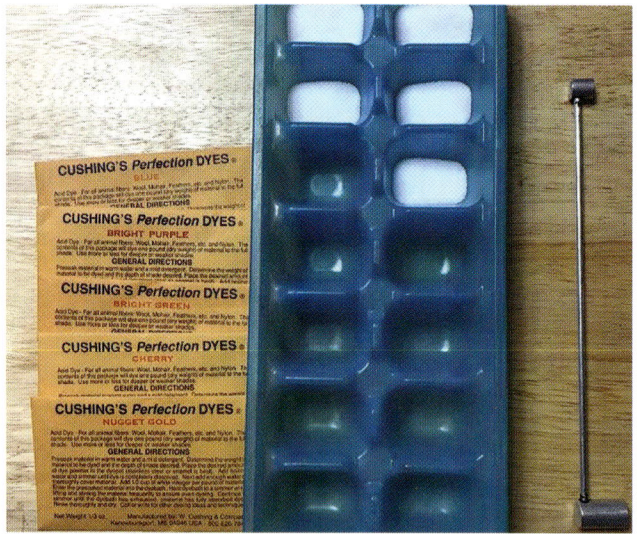

Preparing the dye

Dry dye and salt

Mixing the dry dye and salt

Dry-dyed wool is wonderful. It is as if someone shook a salt shaker of dye all over the wool in a wonderful array of colors. The dry-dyed wool is perfect for impressionist flowers, flower boxes, borders, geometrics, and grasses.

Remember, you will get different looks each time you dry dye, as you cannot sprinkle the dye exactly the same each time. This method of dyeing is fun to do with a few friends. Have everyone prepare a different color and sprinkle away!

Tip!

Try dry dyeing with red acid dyes such as Crimson, Egyptian Red, or Turkey Red coupled with Turquoise and Gold. When hooked up, this wool resembles paisley.

Step-by-Step Lasagna Method Instructions

1. Soak the wool for about 30 minutes prior to dyeing. Add Lemon Joy to open up the fibers.

2. Squeeze excess water from wool.

3. In a flat pan or bottom of a turkey roaster, crumble up foil to create a "rack" so the wool does not cook, but steam. Do not use a real cooking rack as you could burn the wool.

4. Carefully place your wool flat on the foil. The wool may have to be cut to match the foil rack.

5. Mix ⅛ tsp. of your favorite color with 2 tsp. non-iodized salt.

6. Sprinkle ½ tsp. evenly over the front of the wool.

7. Mix a second color the same as the first, and sprinkle ½ tsp. evenly over the front of the wool.

8. Turn the wool over and follow the same process on the back of the wool.

9. Place a second piece of wool on top of the first and repeat the process.

10. Place a third piece of wool on top and repeat the process. Always sprinkle both the front and back of the wool.

11. Pour one cup of hot water into the bottom of the pan. Cover the pan tightly with foil.

12. Bake at 300 degrees in the oven for 45 minutes.

13. Rinse well, and line dry or dry on low heat.

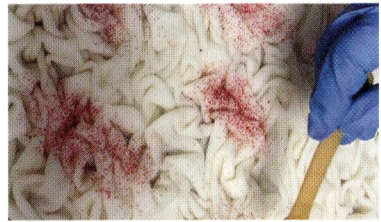

6. Apply the dry dye mixed with salt

10. More of the colors applied

11. Ready to go into the oven

Detail of dry-dye dyed wool

Dry dyed wool, front and back, showing two shades

Hints!

- If you do not sprinkle the dry dye on both sides, you will have one side that will appear white (or whatever color the wool is, if you are dyeing over a pastel).

- If the water is not clear in the pan after 45 minutes, turn off the heat and leave the pan in the oven another 10 minutes.

- Be sure to pour only 1 cup of hot water in the pan. This allows the wool to steam. More than one cup mottles the dry dye.

Dyeing with Kosher Salt

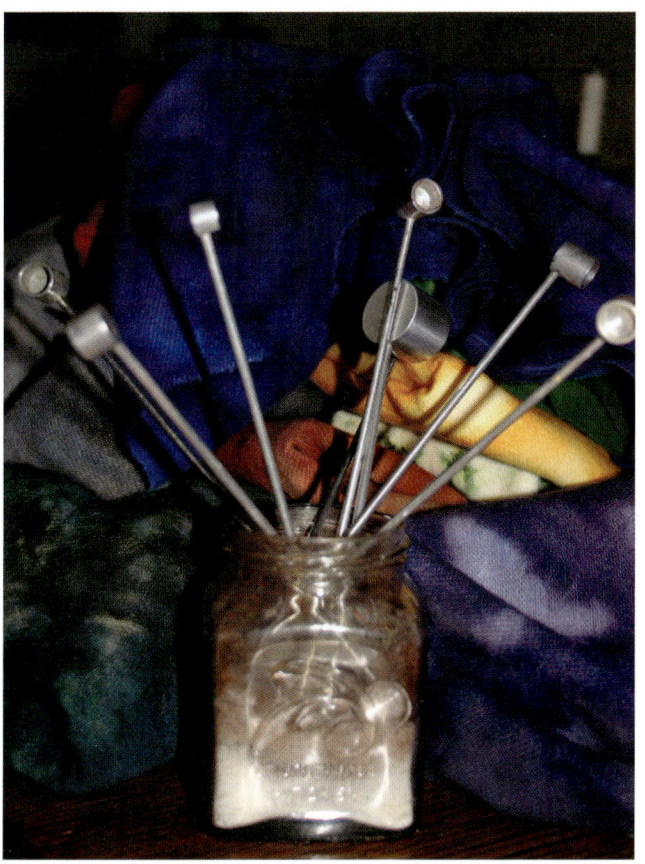

In the dye kitchen, we try to waste as little as possible. If you will remember, in our dye kitchen we keep our dye spoons in a glass jar (an old canning jar) filled with kosher (non-iodized) salt. We put used dye spoons in the jar of salt and turn them a few times to clean the spoons to avoid transferring dye from one dye pot to the next.

Once the salt in the glass jar has turned dark (no white granules showing), you can empty that salt into an airtight glass container and save it for a day when you really want to play in the dye pots. The kosher salt has grabbed little flecks of color every time you cleaned your dye spoons, so your jar of used kosher salt has every color in it that you have used. Your kosher salt jar also tells you just what colors you have used the most.

Dyeing with the kosher salt works best on white, cream, or light gray wools. These wools let the colors come out in a myriad of prisms and a kaleidoscope of color.

So what color wool will you get when you dye with your kosher salt? No one knows, and it is hard to guess. It will be a wonderful sampling of all the colors you have dyed, and since everyone has a different color palette, their kosher salt will dye their wool differently. A true potluck of color!

Why dye with used kosher salt? By dyeing with your used kosher salt, you are using everything in your dye kitchen and not wasting anything. Plus it encourages you to clean your dye spoons and gives you a reason to have a sprinkly fun dye day as you dye with the used kosher salt.

Dyeing with Kosher Salt – What You Need

- Wool: solid and textures, light in color, no more than a yard, presoaked in warm water and a little Lemon Joy
- Used kosher salt
- Enamel or stainless-steel 4-qt. pot
- Dye spoon: 1 tsp.
- 4-cup glass measuring cup
- Citric acid or white vinegar
- Heat source
- Wooden spoon
- Rectangular pan
- Electric kettle

Step-by-Step Dyeing with Kosher Salt Instructions

1. Pre-soak the wool in warm water with a little Lemon Joy to open up the fibers. Soak your wool for a few hours or overnight.

2. The size of your pot depends on the amount of wool you wish to dye. If you use your turkey roaster, use no more than ¾ of a yd. wool.

3. Fill the pot halfway with water.

4. Heat the water to a steam, not a full boil. If you see bubbles in your pot, turn down the heat.

5. Add the soaked wool to the pot; the water should cover the wool. If it does not, add more boiling water.

6. Put 2 tsp. used kosher salt into 4 cups boiling water. Mix thoroughly until the salt is dissolved. This is the dye solution.

7. Pour your dye solution into the steaming pot of water and stir once with a wooden spoon. The more you stir, the less mottled the wool will be. This is your dye bath.

8. Let the wool simmer for 12 to 15 minutes, until the dye bath is almost clear.

9. Add ¼ cup of white vinegar or ¼ tsp. of citric acid. Remove from heat after 3 to 5 minutes; the dye bath water should be clear.

10. Remove your wool from the pot to a separate clean pan.

11. Rinse in cool water and line dry or dry in a dryer on the lowest setting.

8 — How to Make Ugly Wool Pretty

"Ugly wool" is not a color or specific texture. Ugly wool is only ugly in the eyes of the fiber artist. Ugly wool is wool you will not use; it is often a plaid that is too bold or has too much white. But you would use that wool if the color or plaid hooked differently. Well, you can change that wool to make it usable.

This chart shows what you can do with the simple pot-dye method to change your tub of ugly wool into pretty wool for your stash.

LIGHT WOOL

Use with 1 yd. of wool. The dry dye is dissolved in 4 cups boiling water.		
Color of Base Wool	**Dye to Use**	**End Result**
off white	1/32 tsp. Silver Gray Green	soft green
pale gray	1/32 tsp. Reseda Green	soft gray-green
pale pink	1/8 tsp. Green	blue-green
ivory/cream	1/32 tsp. Bronze Green	yellow-green
bright white	1/4 tsp. Khaki Drab	aged green
cream	1/4 tsp. Old Ivory	parchment
oatmeal	1/4 tsp. Champagne	warm orange/peach
pale green	1/8 tsp. Mahogany	rosy beige
cream	1/32 tsp. Egyptian Red	brick
orange	1/4 tsp. Rust	fall leaves
pink	1/8 tsp. Peach	soft peach rose
cream	1/32 tsp. Black	Williamsburg gray-blue
cream	1/32 tsp. Bright Purple	grayed purple
gray	1/32 tsp. Plum	rosy purple
gray	1/8 tsp. Aqua	soft blue

Dark Wool

Use with 1 yd. of wool. The dry dye is dissolved in 4 cups boiling water.		
Color of Base Wool	**Dye to Use**	**End Result**
dark gray	¼ tsp. Dark Green	evergreens
bright green	½ tsp. Golden Brown	glowing brown
bright orange red	½ tsp. Seal Brown	aged red brick
bright blue red	¼ tsp. Mummy Brown	Santa-suit red
maroon	½ tsp. Navy Blue	aged barn siding
plum/eggplant	½ tsp. Peacock	antique black
navy	½ tsp. Turquoise	antique black
black	½ tsp. Turquoise Blue	antique black
aqua	½ tsp. Mahogany	brown red

Textured Wool

Color of Base Wool	Dye to Use	End Result
kelly green plaid	¼ tsp. Mahogany	grass/trees
kelly green plaid	¼ tsp. Navy	ocean/sky
dark green plaid	¼ tsp. Wine	leaves
dark green plaid	¼ tsp. Terra Cotta	hills/leaves
bright blue plaid	¼ tsp. Golden Brown	soft blue-browns
bright yellow plaid	⅛ tsp. Purple	pansies
bright yellow plaid	⅛ tsp. Magenta	roses
purple plaid	½ tsp. Khaki	veins, grapes
scarlet red plaid	½ tsp. Jade	stems
grey/white herringbone	¼ tsp. Purple	tree bark
grey/white herringbone	⅛ tsp. Black	roof shingles
green/white herringbone	¼ tsp. Mummy Brown	fall grass
green/white herringbone	¼ tsp. Khaki	yellow-green

Use with 1 yd. of wool. The dry dye is dissolved in 4 cups boiling water.

Aging Wool

Recipe for Aging Wool

- 1 yd. wool
- ½ tsp. dye in 2 CBW (cup boiling water)
- (This is a heavier concentration of dye than usual because you are aging the wool.)

"Aging" wool means toning it down. If the wool is bright orange red, you can tone it down to a brick red. Or you have bright green wool you want to tone down to an army green. The process you use to age your wool depends on what you would like as the end result. The go-to dyes for aging most wools have been Khaki Drab, Seal Brown, Mummy Brown, and now Black Walnut. Many fiber artists in the past have used real black walnuts, ground to a powder, to dye with or to age their wool. This is messy and time-consuming. Now with the new Black Walnut acid dye, you get the look of aging with black walnuts without the mess.

Khaki Drab gives a green tint to the aging

Mummy Brown gives a rusty tone to the aging

Seal Brown gives a dark brown like mud to the aging

Black Walnut gives a warm brown tone to the aging

9 — What If...? Why Did...? Situations and Solutions

"What if's" and "Why did's?" are a part of dyeing wool—they happen to everyone. Something just did not work out as expected and the dyer is puzzled by the results. What happened here? So let's address some of the most common "Why did's" and "What if's" and I'll give you some possible answers.

1. My wool will not absorb the dye in the dye bath even after citric acid/vinegar has been added.

- Most likely your "wool" is not 100% wool and contains a synthetic content of more than 35 percent.

- You did not soak your wool long enough to open the fibers.

- Your water was not hot enough.

- Some dyes such as red, yellow, or orange take longer to exhaust. You have to make sure your heat is high and add another 10 minutes to the process for these high chroma colors.

- Your dye bath was very rich in color. If you have added 10 more minutes and there is still dye in the dye bath, but your wool when rinsed runs clear, your wool is dyed.

- Let your wool sit overnight in the dye bath to cool completely. More often than not, the dye bath will exhaust overnight.

2. I did not use all of my dye solution. Can I store it? For how long?

- You can store your dye solution in a clean, clear glass jar that seals well. We recommend a mason jar or good jelly jar. Keep the dye solution away from direct light. Your dye solution will be good for up to 6 months.

- When you want to use your stored dye solution, you must reheat the dye solution. You can add ½ cup to 1 cup of boiling water to the stored solution to create the new dye solution. Or you can pour your stored dye solution into your dye pan and add 2 to 3 cups of boiling water for a new dye bath. Bring that to a simmer.

- Be sure to reset your dye solution with either citric acid or white vinegar.

3. My stored dye solution became lumpy when stored.

- Add 2 to 3 cups of boiling water to the dye solution, stir the solution very well, and bring to just below a boil until the solution is smooth. It is best to then set the dye solution with vinegar.

4. I have used the same green dye formula many times; sometimes it is more blueish and sometimes it is more yellowish. What is going on?

- If you have public water, the chlorine content in the water varies as does the fluoride content. These two chemicals will cause variance in your dyed wool.

- If you used more citric acid when dyeing one batch than the other, you might get a difference in color.

- If your base wool is not the same, your color will vary.

5. The dyed wool appears hard or coarse after it is dried.

- You did not simmer the wool; you may have boiled it.

- You used too much citric acid in the dye bath.

Dye Method: Spotty Spot Dye (Aqua, Yellow, Pink, Blue)

Dye Method: Lasagna Method (Bright Purple, American Beauty, Hunter Green, Yellow)

6. My dyed wool has spots of colors I did not add. For instance, my dyed yellow wool has blue or red spots.

- Your dye spoon may not have been cleaned, and it is residue from previous dyeing.

- You did not stir your dye solution thoroughly.

- Your dye pot was not properly cleaned.

7. I ran out of commercial grade citric acid. Can I use the citric acid designed for food?

- You can use the citric acid found in the canning section of the store. However, it is weaker so you may want to use a pinch more.

- You can use white vinegar in its place.

8. I don't like the way my dyed wool turned out. Can I overdye it?

- Yes, you can. Take into consideration the wool has been dyed once, and be careful not to overheat or use too much citric acid or vinegar as your wool might become stiff.

- When you dye over already-dyed wool, be sure your dye formula is strong enough.

9. Can I combine different acid dyes from different manufacturers?

- Yes, you can. You can mix acid dyes from different manufacturers. Be sure your water is boiling when you make your dye solution and be sure to stir the dye solution.

10. I forgot to add the citric acid/vinegar and have dried the wool. Is that okay?

- No. The dye in your wool is not set and could bleed, especially if it is a red. You need to rewet the wool and put it in a dye pot of simmering water. Add citric acid or vinegar. Let the wool simmer for 10–15 minutes.

11. I do not have white or cream wool, but I want to dye.

- Overdye! These are great colors to dye over: pink, pale yellow, pale blues, light grays, peach.

12. After my wool dries, the sides or bottom are still the original color.

- Most likely the wool was folded under when you were dyeing. You need to be sure that the wool is not folded under and the dye is spread evenly.

- You might have run out of dye. If so, mix a second batch because all of the base wool should be covered with dye.

- You did not soak the wool long enough to absorb the dye.

13. When I cut the wool, the center is white.

That is called white core. White core means the dye has not soaked completely into the wool. White core has several causes:

- The water was not hot enough.

- The wool was not presoaked.

- You did not simmer the wool long enough.

- Your wool has more than 35% synthetic content.

14. Why does my wool look different when it is dry?

When your wool is wet in the pan it will appear one to two times darker than when it is dry.

Wet wool in pan

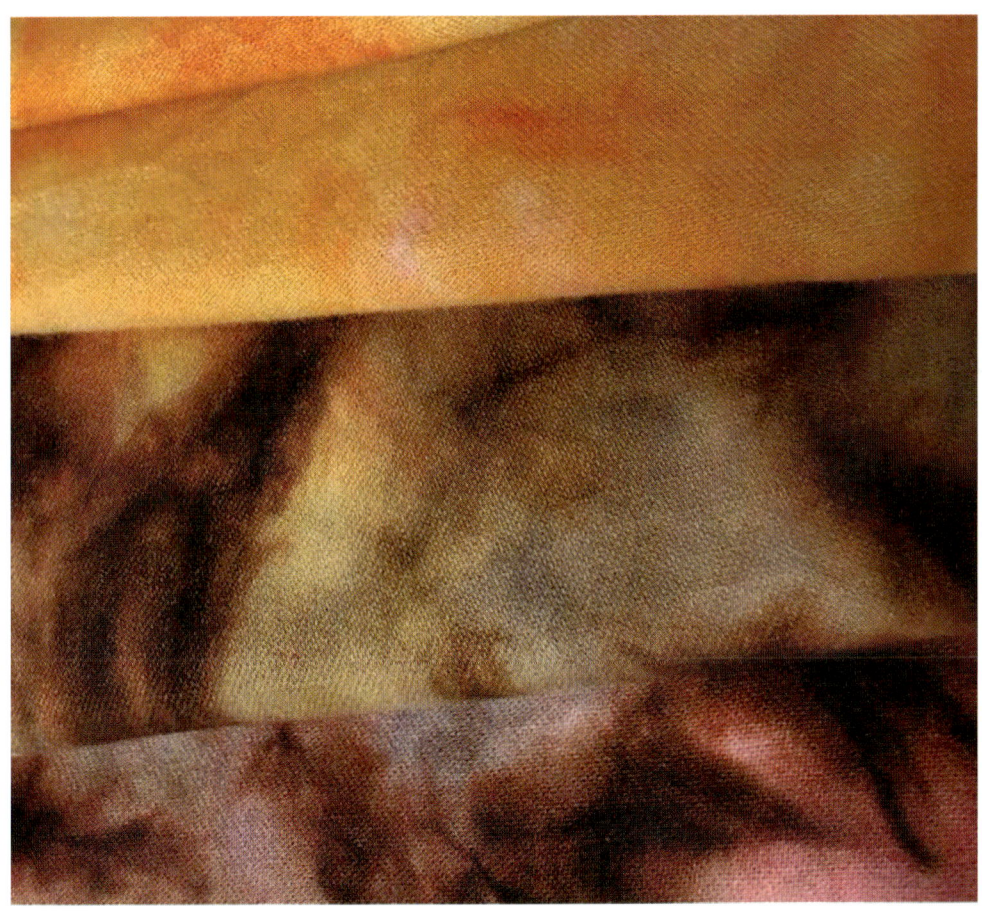

Wool dried and ready to hook

10 — Dye Formulas

Pot Dye/Abrash Formulas

CBW = Cups Boiling Water

Vintage Gold
¼ tsp. Nugget Gold
⅛ tsp. Gold
1/128 tsp. Golden Brown
Mix the three dyes above in 4 CBW. This is your dye solution.

Deep Blue Sea
¼ tsp. Copenhagen Blue
⅛ tsp. Navy
1/128 tsp. Turquoise Blue
Mix the three dyes above in 4 CBW. This is your dye solution.

Nautical Green
⅛ tsp. Jade Green
¼ tsp. Aquagreen
¼ tsp. Nile Green
Mix the three dyes above in 4 CBW. This is your dye solution.

Great Brown Abrash
¼ tsp. Seal Brown
⅛ tsp. Black Walnut
⅛ tsp. Mummy Brown
Mix the three dyes above in 4 CBW. This is your dye solution.

Bricks and More
¼ tsp. Terra Cotta
⅛ tsp. Crimson
Mix the two dyes above in 4 CBW. This is your dye solution.

Peachy Keen
¼ tsp. Peach
⅛ tsp. Coral
⅛ tsp. Salmon
Mix the three dyes above in 4 CBW. This is your dye solution.

Honey Bee
¼ tsp. Buttercup Yellow
⅛ tsp. Yellow
1/32 tsp. Gold
Mix the three dyes above in 4 CBW. This is your dye solution.

Porcelain
¼ tsp. Old Ivory
¼ tsp. Ecru
¼ tsp. Champagne
Mix the three dyes above in 4 CBW. This is your dye solution.

STEP-BY-STEP POT DYE/ABRASH INSTRUCTIONS

Choose a formula and follow these instructions:

1. Pre-soak wool in warm water with a little Lemon Joy to open up the fibers. Soak your wool for a few hours or overnight.

2. The size of pot you need depends on the amount of wool you wish to dye.

3. Fill your pot halfway with water.

4. Bring the pot of water to a steam, not a full boil. If you see bubbles, turn down the heat.

5. Add your soaked wool to the pot, the water should cover the wool. If it does not, add more boiling water.

6. Mix up the chosen dye formula. This is your dye solution.

7. Pour your dye solution into the steaming pot of water and stir once with a wooden spoon. The more you stir, the less mottled the wool will be. This is the dye bath.

8. Let the wool simmer for 12 to 15 minutes, until the dye bath is almost clear.

9. Add ¼ cup of white vinegar or ¼ tsp. of citric acid and simmer 3 to 5 minutes. The dye bath water should be clear.

10. Remove your wool from the pot into a separate clean pan.

11. Rinse in cool water and line dry or dry in a dryer on the lowest setting.

DIP DYE FORMULAS

Basic dip dye step by step:

1. Bring a 2-qt. pot of water half full to a steam, not a full boil. The pot should have 8 to 12 cups of water.

2. Pour dye solution into the pot of water and stir thoroughly.

3. Begin dip dyeing in the dye bath with about 3 inches in the pot. In a dipping fashion, slowly dip 8 to 10 times and move up the quarter yard of wool.

4. When you get to the top of the wool, take the top 3 inches (allowing overlap) and drape it over your wooden spoon. Now quickly dip the top of the wool that is not yet dyed, one or two times, to fill in the lightest color.

5. Remove the dip dyed wool from the pot into a separate pan.

6. Rinse your wool in cool water and dry.

7. If the pot still has color and is not exhausted, repeat the same procedure with a second piece of wool for a lighter highlight wool.

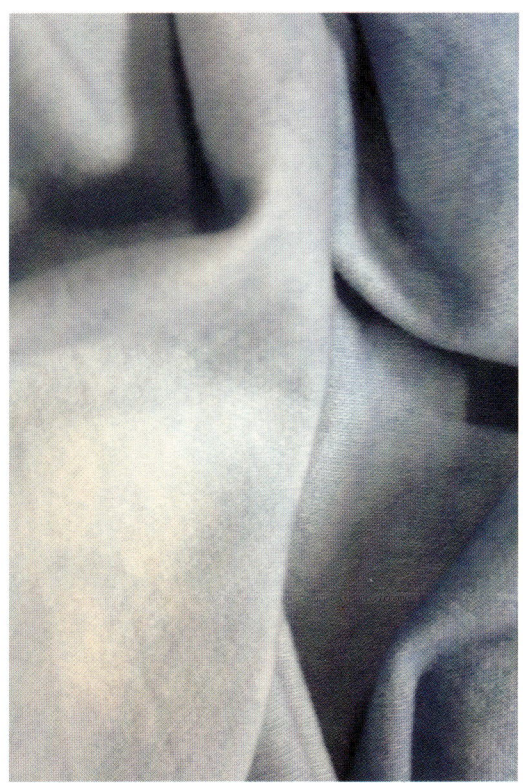

Dip Dye Green Stems
¼ tsp. Hunter Green in 2 CBW plus ¼ tsp. citric acid
¼ yard white or cream wool, pre-soaked

Dip Dye Day Lilies
Mix these three dyes in 4 CBW plus ¼ tsp. citric acid:
⅛ tsp. Orange
1/32 tsp. Coral
1/64 tsp. Peach
¼ yard white or cream wool, pre-soaked

Dip Dye Ocean Waves
Mix these three dyes in 4 CBW plus ¼ tsp. citric acid:
1/64 tsp. Turquoise Blue
1/64 tsp. Peacock
1/128 tsp. Sky Blue
½ yard white or cream wool, pre-soaked

Dip Dye Grapes
Mix these three dyes in 4 CBW plus ¼ tsp. citric acid:
1/32 tsp. Purple
1/64 tsp. Bright Purple
1/128 tsp. Lavender
¼ yard white or cream wool, pre-soaked

Dip Dye Very Berry
Mix these three dyes in 4 CBW plus ¼ tsp. citric acid:
1/32 tsp. Strawberry
1/64 tsp. Redgrape
1/128 tsp. Garnet
¼ yard white or cream wool, pre-soaked

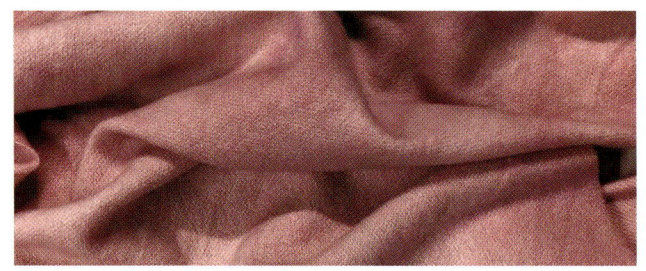

Double-Color Dip Dyes

Choose a recipe and follow these basic dip dye directions.

STEP-BY-STEP DOUBLE-COLOR DIP DYEING INSTRUCTIONS

1. Bring two 2-qt. pots of water half full to a steam, not a full boil. The pots should have 10–12 cups of water.

2. Pour Dye Pot #1 dye solution into the first pot of water and stir thoroughly.

3. Pour Dye Pot #2 dye solution into the second pot of water and stir thoroughly.

4. Begin dip dyeing in the dye bath of Dye Pot #1 with about 3 inches in the pot. In a dipping fashion, slowly dip 8 to 10 times, and move up the strip of wool.

5. When you get to the top of the wool, take the top 5 inches (allowing overlap) and drape it over your wooden spoon. Now quickly dip the top of the wool that is not yet dyed, one or two times into Dye Pot #2 until the color is filled in.

6. Move the dip dyed wool from the pot to a separate pan.

7. Rinse the wool in cool water and dry.

8. If the pots still have color and are not exhausted, repeat the same procedure with a second quarter yard of wool for a lighter highlight wool. Also, you can reverse the double dip dye and start in Dye Pot #2 and move to Dye Pot #1.

Double-Color Dip Dye Coneflower

Dye Pot #1: Mix these three dyes in 4 CBW plus ¼ tsp. citric acid:
¼ tsp. Rose
¼ tsp. Pink
⅛ tsp. Cherry
½ yard white or cream wool, pre-soaked

Dye Pot #2: Mix these two dyes in 4 CBW plus ¼ tsp. citric acid:
¼ tsp. Canary
⅛ tsp. Yellow
1 yard of white or cream wool, pre-soaked

Double-Color Dip Dye Blushing Colors

Dye Pot #1: Mix these three dyes in 4 CBW plus ¼ tsp. citric acid:
¼ tsp. Aqualon Pink
¼ tsp. Pink
⅛ tsp. Rose Pink
½ yard white or cream wool, pre-soaked

Dye Pot #2: Mix these two dyes in 4 CBW plus ¼ tsp. citric acid:
¼ tsp. Aqualon Yellow
⅛ tsp. Lemon
1 yard of white or cream wool, pre-soaked

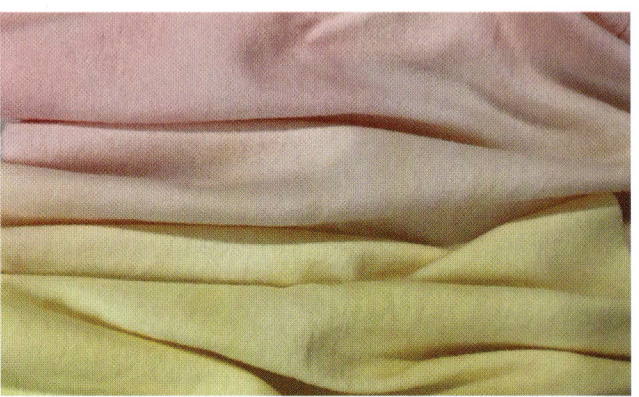

Double-Color Dip Dye Winding Road

Dye Pot #1: Mix these three dyes in 4 CBW plus ¼ tsp. citric acid:
¼ tsp. Dark Brown
¼ tsp. Spice Brown
1/128 tsp. Mummy Brown
½ yard white or cream wool, pre-soaked

Dye Pot #2: Mix these two dyes in 4 CBW plus ¼ tsp. citric acid:
¼ tsp. Khaki Drab
1/32 tsp. Silver Gray Green
1 yard of white or cream wool, pre-soaked

Spot Dye Formulas

Spot Dye: Greens of the Forest
¼ tsp. Green in 4 CBW
¼ tsp. Hunter Green in 4 CBW
¼ tsp. Reseda Green in 4 CBW

Step-by-Step Instructions

1. Wet 1 yd. of white or cream-colored wool. Place wet wool into pan, scrunched to fit.

2. Spot dye in the order above, making sure no white wool is left uncovered. Fill in white spots with any remaining Reseda Green.

3. Mix ½ cup vinegar with ½ cup warm water, pour all over spot dye. Heat on medium to medium high heat for 20 minutes or until water clears.

4. Rinse and dry.

Spot Dye: Falling Leaves
⅛ tsp. Bronze in 4 CBW
⅛ tsp. Dark Green in 4 CBW
⅛ tsp. Golden Brown in 4 CBW

Step-by-Step Instructions

1. Wet ½ yard of white, cream, or yellow colored wool. Place wet wool into pan making sure the wool does not overlap but is "scrunched."

2. Spot dye in the order above, making sure no wool is left uncovered. Fill in white spots with any remaining Bronze.

3. Mix ½ cup vinegar with ½ cup warm water, pour all over spot dye. Heat on medium to medium high heat for 20 minutes or until water clears.

4. Rinse and dry.

Note!

¼ tsp. citric acid dissolved into ½ cup warm water can be substituted for the vinegar in any dye recipe.

Spot Dye: Fall

1/64 tsp. Canary in 2 CBW
1/64 tsp. Turkey Red in 2 CBW
1/64 tsp. Purple in 2 CBW
1/64 tsp. Khaki Drab in 2 CBW

Step-by-Step Instructions

1. Wet ½ yard of white, cream, or sparkle colored wool. Place wet wool into pan making sure the wool does not overlap; scrunch to fit.

2. Spot dye in the order above, making sure no wool is left uncolored. Fill in white spots with any remaining Khaki.

3. Mix ½ cup vinegar with ½ cup warm water, pour all over spot dye. Heat on medium to medium high for 20 minutes or until water clears.

4. Rinse and dry.

Spot Dye: Sky

¼ tsp. Aqualon Blue in 4 CBW
⅛ tsp. Baby Blue in 4 CBW

Step-by-Step Instructions

1. Wet ½ yard of white, cream, or sparkle colored wool. Place wet wool into pan making sure the wool does not overlap; scrunch to fit.

2. Spot dye in the order above, making sure no wool is left uncolored. Fill in white spots with any remaining Baby Blue.

3. Mix ½ cup vinegar with ½ cup warm water, pour all over spot dye. Heat on medium to medium high for 20 minutes or until water clears.

4. Rinse and dry.

Note!

¼ tsp. citric acid dissolved into ½ cup warm water can be substituted for the vinegar in any dye recipe.

Spot Dye: Fall Pumpkin Patch
⅛ tsp. of Orange in 2 CBW
⅛ tsp. of Chartreuse in 2 CBW
⅛ tsp. of Nugget Gold in 2 CBW
⅛ tsp. of Myrtle Green in 2 CBW

Step-by-Step Instructions

1. Wet ½ yard of white, cream, or sparkle colored wool. Place wet wool into pan making sure the wool does not overlap; scrunch to fit.

2. Spot dye in the order above, making sure no wool is left uncolored. Fill in white spots with any remaining Orange or Chartreuse.

3. Mix ½ cup vinegar with ½ cup warm water, pour all over spot dye. Heat on medium to medium high for 20 minutes or until water clears.

4. Rinse and dry.

Spot Dye: Sangria
⅛ tsp. Magenta in 4 CBW
1/32 tsp. Wine in 4 CBW
1/32 tsp. Mulberry in 2 CBW
1/64 tsp. Redgrape in 2 CBW

Step-by-Step Instructions

1. Wet 1 yd. of white, cream, or pink colored wool. Place wet wool into pan making sure the wool does not overlap; scrunch to fit.

2. Spot dye in the order above, making sure no wool is left uncovered. Fill in empty spots with any remaining Mulberry or Redgrape.

3. Mix ½ cup vinegar with ½ cup warm water, pour all over spot dye. Heat on medium to medium high heat for 20 minutes or until water clears.

4. Rinse and dry.

Note!

¼ tsp. citric acid dissolved into ½ cup warm water can be substituted for the vinegar in any dye recipe.

Spot Dye: Oh La La Red
⅛ tsp. American Beauty in 4 CBW
⅛ tsp. Turkey Red in 4 CBW
⅛ tsp. Cardinal in 4 CBW

Step-by-Step Instructions

1. Wet ½ yard of white, cream, or pink colored wool. Place wet wool into pan making sure the wool does not overlap; scrunch to fit.

2. Spot dye in the order above, making sure no wool is left uncovered. Fill in white spots with any remaining American Beauty.

3. Mix ½ cup vinegar with ½ cup warm water, pour all over spot dye. Heat on medium to medium high heat for 20 minutes or until water clears.

4. Rinse and dry.

Spot Dye: Dirty Patch
¼ tsp. Mummy Brown in 4 CBW
¼ tsp. Seal Brown in 4 CBW
¹⁄₃₂ tsp. Golden Brown in 2 CBW

Step-by-Step Instructions

1. Wet ½ yard of white, cream, or pink colored wool. Place wet wool into pan making sure the wool does not overlap; scrunch to fit.

2. Spot dye in the order above, making sure no wool is left uncovered. Fill in white spots with any remaining Golden Brown.

3. Mix ½ cup vinegar with ½ cup warm water, pour all over spot dye. Heat on medium to medium high heat for 20 minutes or until water clears.

4. Rinse and dry.

Note!

¼ tsp. citric acid dissolved into ½ cup warm water can be substituted for the vinegar in any dye recipe.

Casserole and Spot Dyeing Formulas

Oak Leaves
¼ tsp. Wine in 2 CBW
¼ tsp. Salmon in 2 CBW
¼ tsp. Light Brown in 2 CBW

Step-by-Step Instructions

1. Wet ½ yard of white or cream-colored wool. Place wet wool into pan making sure the wool does not overlap.

2. Spot dye or casserole dye in the order above, making sure no white wool is left uncovered. Fill in white spots with any remaining Light Brown.

3. Mix ½ cup vinegar with ½ cup warm water, pour all over spot dye. Heat on medium to medium high heat for 20 minutes or until water clears.

4. Rinse and dry.

Foliage
¼ tsp. Golden Brown in 2 CBW
¼ tsp. Chartreuse in 2 CBW
⅛ tsp. Scarlet in 2 CBW

Step-by-Step Instructions

1. Wet ½ yard of white, cream, or yellow wool. Place wet wool into pan making sure the wool does not overlap.

2. Spot or casserole dye in the order above, making sure no wool is left uncovered. Fill in white spots with any remaining chartreuse.

3. Mix ½ cup vinegar with ½ cup warm water, pour all over spot dye. Heat on medium to medium high heat for 20 minutes or until water clears.

4. Rinse and dry.

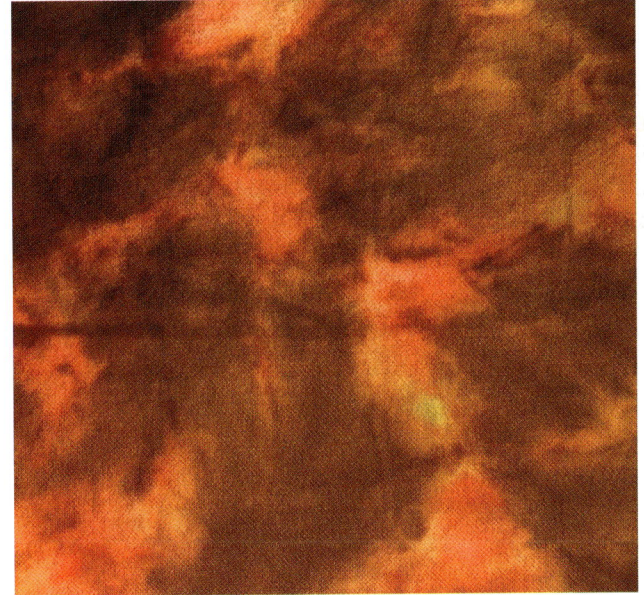

Note!

¼ tsp. citric acid dissolved into ½ cup warm water can be substituted for the vinegar in any dye recipe.

Spring

⅛ tsp. Bronze Green in 2 CBW
¼ tsp. Chartreuse in 2 CBW
¼ tsp. Khaki Drab in 2 CBW

Step-by-Step Instructions

1. Wet ½ yard of white, cream, light green, or yellow colored wool. Place wet wool into pan making sure the wool does not overlap.

2. Spot dye in the order above, making sure no wool is left uncovered. Fill in white spots with any remaining Bronze Green.

3. Mix ½ cup vinegar with ½ cup warm water, pour all over spot dye. Heat on medium to medium high heat for 20 minutes or until water clears.

4. Rinse and dry.

Summer

¼ tsp. Green in 1 CBW
¼ tsp. Olive Green in 1 CBW
⅛ tsp. Ocean Green in 1 CBW

Step-by-Step Instructions

1. Wet ½ yard of white, cream, pink, or blue wool. Place wet wool into pan making sure the wool does not overlap.

2. Spot dye or casserole dye in the order above, making sure no wool is left uncovered. Fill in white spots with any remaining Ocean Green.

3. Mix ½ cup vinegar with ½ cup warm water, pour all over spot dye. Heat on medium to medium high heat for 20 minutes or until water clears.

4. Rinse and dry.

Note!

¼ tsp. citric acid dissolved into ½ cup warm water can be substituted for the vinegar in any dye recipe.

Sunrise/Sunset
⅛ tsp. Coral in 2 CBW
⅛ tsp. Maize in 2 CBW
⅛ tsp. Nile in 2 CBW

Step-by-Step Instructions

1. Wet ½ yard of white, cream, or blue colored wool. Place wet wool into pan, making sure the wool does not overlap.

2. Spot dye or casserole dye in the order above, making sure no wool is left uncovered. Fill in white spots with any remaining Coral.

3. Mix ½ cup vinegar with ½ cup warm water, pour all over spot dye. Heat on medium to medium high heat for 20 minutes or until water clears.

4. Rinse and dry.

Evergreens
⅛ tsp. Black in 2 CBW
⅛ tsp. Dark Green in 2 CBW
¼ tsp. Myrtle Green in 2 CBW

Step-by-Step Instructions

1. Wet ½ yard of white, cream, or pink colored wool. Place wet wool into pan making sure the wool does not overlap.

2. Spot dye or casserole dye in the order above, making sure no wool is left uncovered. Fill in white spots with any remaining Dark Green.

3. Mix ½ cup vinegar with ½ cup warm water, pour all over spot dye. Heat on medium to medium high heat for 20 minutes or until water clears.

4. Rinse and dry.

Note!

¼ tsp. citric acid dissolved into ½ cup warm water can be substituted for the vinegar in any dye recipe.

Lake

⅛ tsp. Turquoise Blue in 2 CBW
⅛ tsp. Silver Gray in 1 CBW
⅛ tsp. Old Ivory in 1 CBW

Step-by-Step Instructions

1. Wet ½ yard of white, cream, or gray colored wool. Place wet wool into pan, making sure the wool does not overlap.

2. Spot dye or casserole dye in the order above, making sure no wool is left uncovered. Fill in white spots with any remaining Silver Gray.

3. Mix ½ cup vinegar with ½ cup warm water, pour all over spot dye. Heat on medium to medium high heat for 20 minutes or until water clears.

4. Rinse and dry.

Shadows

1/16 tsp. Black in 2 CBW
⅛ tsp. in 2 CBW
⅛ tsp. in 2 CBW

Step-by-Step Instructions

1. Wet ½ yard of white or cream-colored wool. Place wet wool into pan making sure the wool does not overlap.

2. Spot dye in the order above, making sure no wool is left uncovered. Fill in white spots with any remaining Aqua.

3. Mix ½ cup vinegar with ½ cup warm water, pour all over spot dye. Heat on medium to medium high heat for 20 minutes or until water clears.

4. Rinse and dry.

Note!

¼ tsp. citric acid dissolved into ½ cup warm water can be substituted for the vinegar in any dye recipe.

Snow and Ice Dyeing Formulas

(These formulas can also be used in the pot dye method, casserole dyeing method, yarn dyeing, and spot dye method.)

Bold Fun
¼ tsp. Turquoise Green
⅛ tsp. Peacock
¼ tsp. Jade Green
Mix each of the above in 2 CBW. This is your dye solution.

Tricolor Fun
¼ tsp. Cherry
⅛ tsp. Orchid
⅛ tsp. Aquagreen
Mix each of the above in 2 CBW. These are your dye solutions. Pour separately like a spot dye.

Bubble Gum
⅛ tsp. Pink
¼ tsp. Rose Pink
1/128 tsp. Flower Power Pink
Mix each of the above in 2 CBW. These are your dye solutions. Pour separately like a spot dye.

Vintage
¼ tsp. Old Gold
⅛ tsp. Bronze
1/32 tsp. Khaki
Mix each of the above in 2 CBW. These are your dye solutions. Pour separately like a spot dye.

Dye Formulas | 99

Soft and Sweet
¼ tsp. Salmon
¼ tsp. Apricot
¼ tsp. Peach
Mix each of the above in 2 CBW. These are your dye solutions. Pour separately like a spot dye.

Lipstick Red
¼ tsp. American Beauty
⅛ tsp. Turkey Red
⅛ tsp. Aqualon Wine
Mix each of the above in 2 CBW. These are your dye solutions. Pour separately like a spot dye.

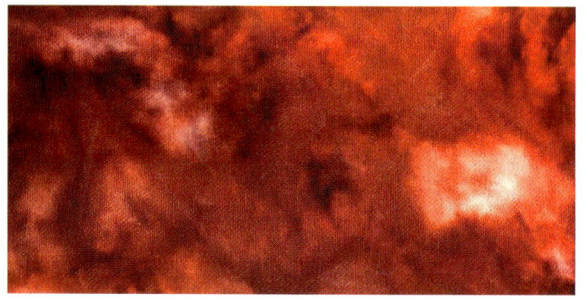

Winter Grays
¼ tsp. Silver Gray
⅛ tsp. Dark Gray
1/128 tsp. Silver Gray Green
Mix each of the above in 2 CBW. These are your dye solutions. Pour separately like a spot dye.

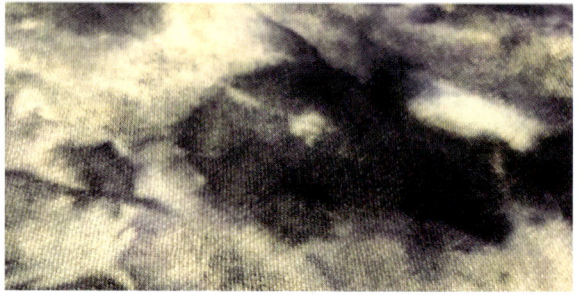

Daffodil
¼ tsp. Yellow
¼ tsp. Buttercup Yellow
1/32 tsp. Maize
Mix each of the above in 2 CBW. These are your dye solutions. Pour separately like a spot dye.

Dye Method: Abrash (Mummy Brown, Seal Brown, Dark Gray)

Yarn Dyeing Formulas

Choose one of these formulas and follow the instructions in the Yarn Dyeing Chapter.

(These formulas can also be used in the pot dye method, casserole dyeing method, yarn dyeing, and spot dye method.)

Purple
¼ tsp. Bright Purple
⅛ tsp. Lavender
Mix the two dyes above in 4 CBW. This is your dye solution.

Red Berry
¼ tsp. Cherry
⅛ tsp. Mulberry
Mix the two dyes above in 4 CBW. This is your dye solution.

Grassy Green
⅛ tsp. Hunter Green
¼ tsp. Bright Green
¼ tsp. Green
Mix the three dyes above in 4 CBW. This is your dye solution.

Antique Black
¼ tsp. Burgundy
⅛ tsp. Peacock
¹⁄₃₂ tsp. Black
Mix the three dyes above in 4 CBW. This is your dye solution.

Fall Grass
¼ tsp. Khaki
⅛ tsp. Khaki Drab
Mix the two dyes above in 4 CBW. This is your dye solution.

Warm Brown Betty
¼ tsp. Golden Brown
⅛ tsp. Medium Brown
⅛ tsp. Light Brown
Mix the three dyes above in 4 CBW. This is your dye solution.

Oriental Red
¼ tsp. Crimson
⅛ tsp. Cardinal
⅛ tsp. Egyptian Red
Mix the three dyes above in 4 CBW. This is your dye solution.

Spring Blue
¼ tsp. Robin's Egg Blue
¼ tsp. Baby Blue
¼ tsp. Aqua
Mix the three dyes above in 4 CBW. This is your dye solution.

Dye Method: Abrash (Granite, Silver Gray)

Dye Method: Spotty Spot Dye (Granite, Silver Gray, Rust)

Dye Formulas | 107

IMARI FORMULAS

By Joan Moshimer

The Imari dye formulas are beautiful in their depth of color, especially when they are spot dyed. These are the formulas which were developed by Joan Moshimer in the 1970s for particular use in Oriental rugs. Many people through the years have tried to reproduce these through trial and error, with varying success. These are Joan's original formulas, and can be used with the other dye methods in this book: spot dye, dip dye, or swatch dyeing.

Imari Dyeing – What You Need

- ½ yd. pieces natural wool, soaked in warm water with Lemon Joy
- Dyes: Blue, Navy Blue, Royal Blue, Crimson, Egyptian Red, Apricot, and Gold
- All of these formulas require 2 cups boiling water

- Acid dyes for the Imari colors
- Enamel or stainless-steel flat pan, 16" x 24" or smaller
- Dye spoons: ¼ tsp. and ½ tsp.
- One 4-cup glass measuring cup
- Two 2-cup glass measuring cups
- Metal tablespoon
- White vinegar
- Heat source
- Wooden spoon
- Rectangular pan for wool to cool

Below: **Havrah Oreintal.** *Imari formulas used: Imari Blue 1, Imari Gray, Imari Red 1, Imari Gold 1.*

Imari Instructions

1. Pre-soak your wool in warm water and use a little Lemon Joy. This will open the fibers. Let it soak for a few hours or even overnight.

2. Let the wool drain in the sink. Do not squeeze out excess water.

3. Prepare the Imari dye recipe:

   - Mix the dye solution in the 4-cup measuring cup, add boiling water.

   - Split the 4-cup dye solution into two 2-cup measuring cups. This allows you to pour more evenly and get great mottling.

4. Take your wet wool, and without wringing it out, place it in the bottom of the large flat pan. It will be much too large to fit flat in the pan, so with both hands, manipulate it to fit: distribute the cloth as evenly as you can. Be sure your wool is wrinkled and arranged evenly.

5. Take some time with this step. It is this wrinkling that will make the beautiful patterns when you apply the dyes. The smaller the pan is, the more time you will have to take to tuck the wool down so it is distributed as evenly as possible. Relax and take your time—this is an important step.

6. With a tablespoon, spoon the dye in the first 2-cup measure onto the wool in spots about the size of a medium apple, 2" to 3" apart. (Use about 1½ to 2 cups of the dye solution. Keep the leftover dye solution to fill in white spots at the end.) Important: use the back of the tablespoon to blend the main color spots into the wool.

7. Now spoon the second 2-cup measure of mixed dye onto the wool in the spaces next to the main color. Make sure you use the back of the tablespoon to blend the main color into the secondary color so they mix and all the wool between them is covered with dye solution. (Use a little over 1½ cups of the dye solution in this step.)

8. With the tablespoon, carefully spoon remaining dye solution onto the wool in the blank spaces or blended spaces between the main and secondary colors. Using the back of the spoon, blend all colors together carefully so that no white or cream wool shows. Take your time with this: be sure the entire piece of wool is covered before you go to the next step.

9. Pour ½ cup vinegar over the entire pan of wool.

10. Pour 1 cup of water over the entire pan of wool. This will ensure mottling and blending.

11. Let the wool simmer (not boil) for 25 to 30 minutes or until the water under the dyed wool is clear. If you need to, add a little more water—do not let the water evaporate from the pan or you will burn the wool.

12. Remove the wool from the pan and place in a clean pan. A good pan to use is a square enamel or stainless-steel pan. Let the wool cool for 10 to 15 minutes.

13. Rinse the wool in cool (not cold) water. (Cold water may shock the wool and could cause the wool to felt.) Line dry or dry in a dryer on the lowest setting.

Imari Blue #1

1 tsp. Royal Blue

¼ tsp. Blue

¹⁄₃₂ tsp. Egyptian Red

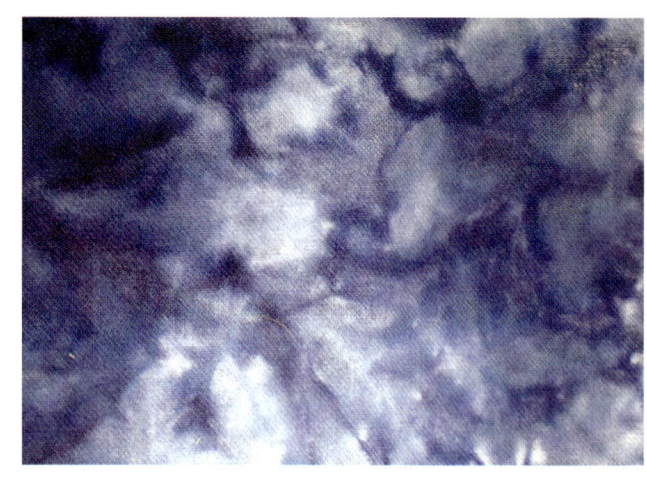

Imari Blue #2

½ tsp. Blue

¼ tsp. Navy Blue

¹⁄₁₆ tsp. Crimson

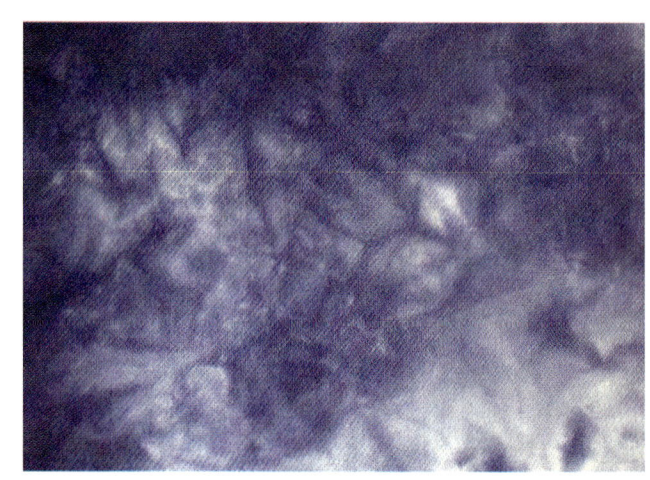

Imari Gray (a soft green-gray)

¼ tsp. Blue

¼ tsp. Gold

¹⁄₃₂ tsp. Egyptian Red

Imari Red #1
1 tsp. Egyptian Red
¼ tsp. Crimson
⅟₃₂ tsp. Royal Blue

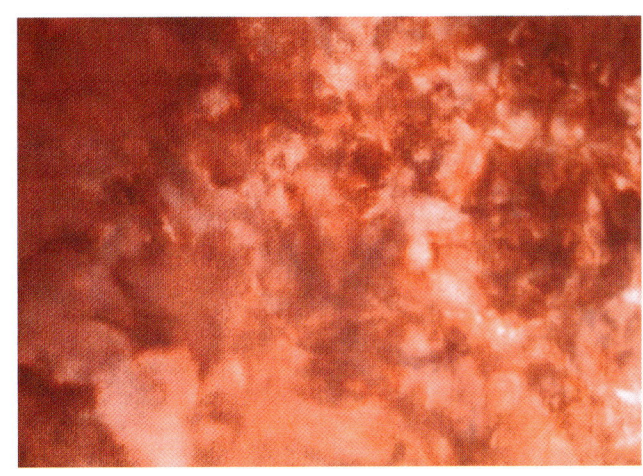

Imari Red #2 (bright red)
1 tsp. Crimson
½ tsp. Apricot
⅟₃₂ tsp. Blue

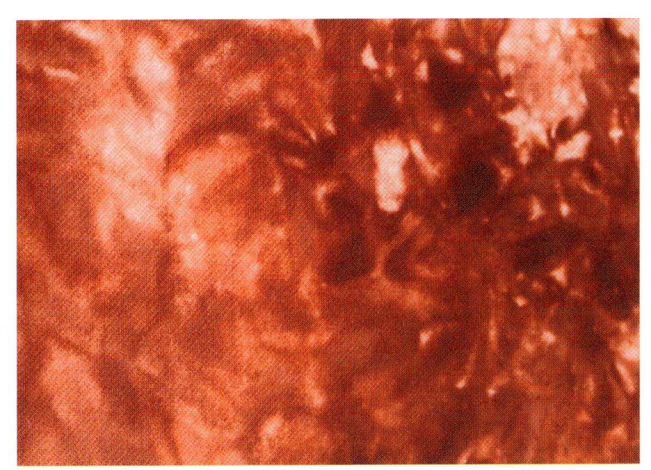

Imari Rose Taupe (soft, grayed)
¼ tsp. Egyptian Red
¼ tsp. Blue
⅛ tsp. Gold

Imari Gold #1

½ tsp. Gold

½ tsp. Apricot

⅟₃₂ tsp. Blue

⅟₃₂ tsp. Egyptian Red

Imari Gold #2

1 tsp. Gold

⅟₃₂ tsp. Blue

⅟₃₂ tsp. Egyptian Red

Imari Brown (golden brown)

½ tsp. Apricot

¼ tsp. Blue

⅟₃₂ tsp. Egyptian Red

Imari Jade Green

½ tsp. Blue

¾ tsp. Gold

¹⁄₁₆ tsp. Apricot

Imari Chinese Green

½ tsp. Gold

⅛ tsp. Blue

¹⁄₃₂ tsp. Apricot

Imari Violet

½ tsp. Crimson

¼ plus ¹⁄₁₆ tsp. Blue

¹⁄₃₂ tsp. Gold

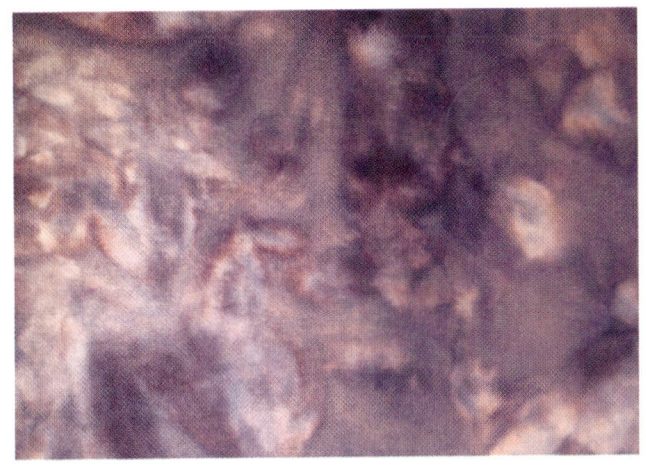

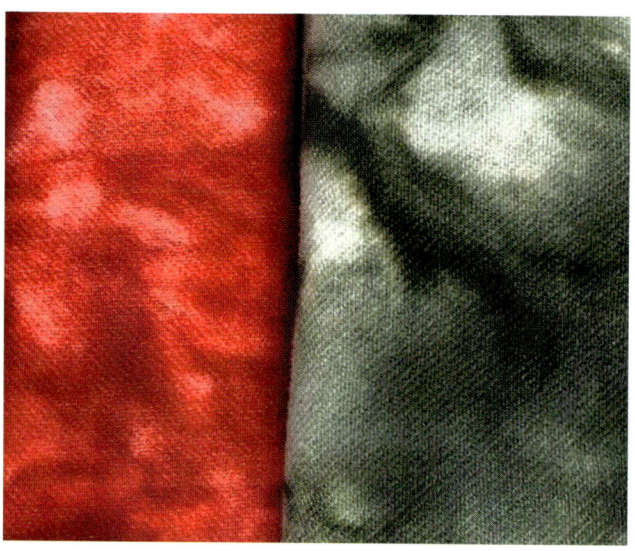

Imari Red #1 spot dyed on left; Imari Jade Green spot dyed on right

Detail of **Cumberland Crewel**

Detail of **Cumberland Crewel.** Imari formulas used: Imari Blue #1 and 2, Imari Gray, Imari Rose Taupe, Imari Brown, Imari Red #2.

Dye Over Colored Wool For A Variety Of Colors

Remember that by dyeing over colored wools (instead of white or natural wool), you will widen your range of hues considerably, and they will all be harmonious.

For instance, dye either of the reds or golds over yellow or orange wools for some light, bright hues. Or dye either of the reds over a light brown or medium green wool for
deeper, duller reds.

Likewise, by dyeing either of the blues over lavender wool, you will get blues that are much more purple-blue.

And the greens, dyed over light and medium yellow-green wools, or dyed over light and medium blue wools, will give you delightful colors. If you want very dull greens, dye over pink or rose-colored wool.

Glossary

⅛ yard: piece of material measuring 9" x 15"

abrash: a technique that produces a mottled look, found in antique rugs

acid dye: dye suitable for wool, mohair, and nylon

antique black: a black that has been worn, mottled, and has a shine due to age and use

CBW: cup boiling water

citric acid: used to set the dye to the wool

crowded pot: a pot of dyed wool with very little water to circulate around the wool

dip dyeing: dyeing to achieve the darkest value to lightest value of one or more colors on one piece of wool, without any hard, defining lines

direct dye: dye suitable for cottons and cellulose materials, plus linen and rayon

dye bath: the vessel of simmering water that contains the dye solution

dye formula: your recipe of how much dye, what colors, and how much water the dye is dissolved in

dye pot: the vessel of simmering water that contains the dye solution

dye solution: the boiling water and dry mix dyes that you will pour into the simmering water to create the dye bath

exhaust: when your dye bath water is clear or almost clear, the dye has "exhausted"

fat quarter: piece of material measuring 18" x 30"

simmer: temperature just below boiling, steam will rise but no bubbles should appear

skein: a length of yarn loosely coiled and knotted

skinny fat quarter: piece of material 9" x 60"

spot dyeing: three colors poured over wool to make a varied and colorful wool

swatch: usually several pieces of dyed wool of one color, from the darkest value to the lightest value of that color

Tbsp.: tablespoon

textured wool: wool that is not solid colored; it can be striped, checked, plaid, or herringbone

tsp.: teaspoon

union dye: Original Perfection Dyes, from Wainwright Cushing that were multi-use and were called "ordinary" Perfection Dyes. Developed after the Civil War

value: the lightness or darkness of a color

white core: when you cut into a piece of dyed wool and the center is white. This means that the wool was not left in the dye bath long enough for the dye to absorb through the entire thickness of material.

white vinegar: used to set the dye to the wool

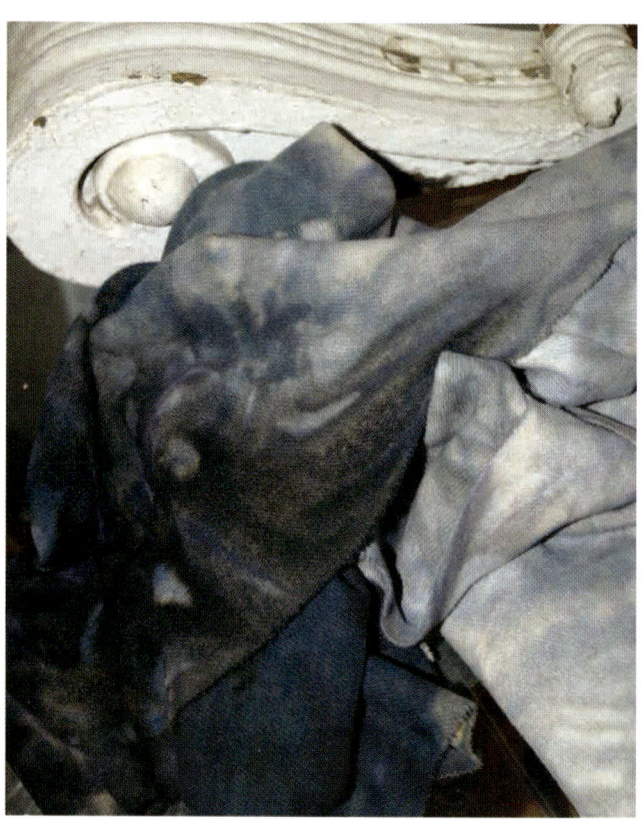

Dedication
To Ron, Tucker and in loving memory of Dick LaBarge.

Acknowledgments
My sincere thanks to each and every person who encouraged, nurtured and fostered my love of the dye pots. First and foremost Dick LaBarge, who gave a very young rug hooker a dye spoon, white wool, and a few dyes, then said, "Let's get on with it."

Sincere gratitude to the many people without whose help this book would not have been possible. To my "big sisters" –Jessie, Roz, and Evelyn—who foster and guide. My "sous chefs" in the dye kitchen Gloria Pierce and Donna Hansen. Debra Smith who kept me on task during difficult times. Joan Moshimer, Ruth Hall, and Annie Spring who laid the foundation so many years ago.

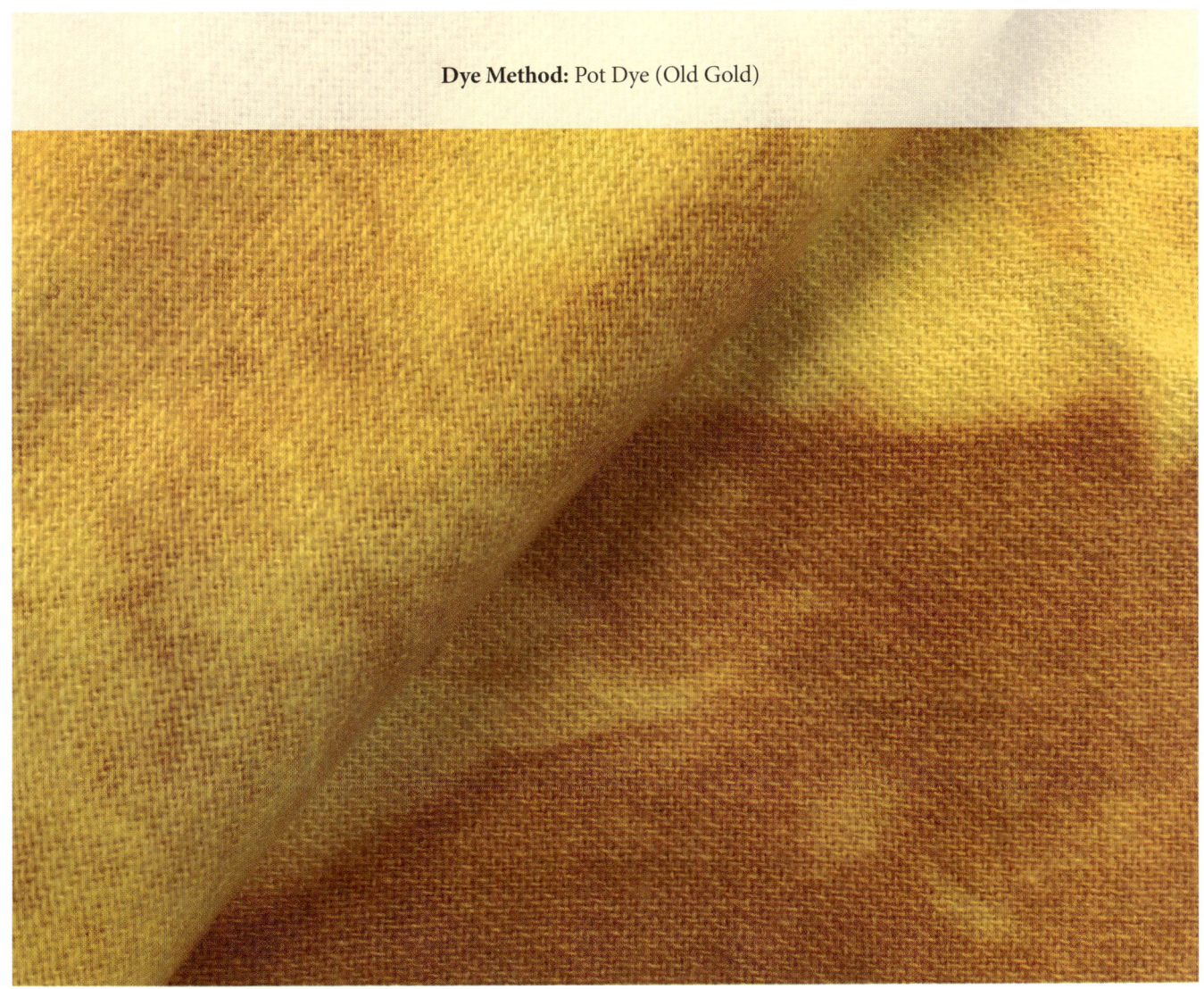

Dye Method: Pot Dye (Old Gold)

Dye Formulas | 117

Dye Method: Pot Dye (Navy Blue)

Dye Methods: Beautifully Blended Spot Dye and Spotty Spot Dye

Dye Formulas | 119

My Dyeing Notes

Limited-Time Offer! Get Your FREE Copy Hot Off the Press!

RUG HOOKING

Join the premium community for rug hookers! Claim your FREE, no-risk issue of *Rug Hooking* Magazine.

Sign up to receive your free trial issue (a $11.95 value).

Love the magazine? Simply pay the invoice for one full year (4 more issues for a total of 5).

Don't love the magazine? No problem! Keep the free issue as our special gift to you, and you owe absolutely nothing!

Claim Your FREE Trial Issue Today!

Sign up online at www.rughookingmagazine.com/BWFC20

Call us toll-free to subscribe at (877) 297 - 0965

Canadian customers call (866) 375 - 8626

Use PROMO Code: **BWFC20**

 -

Discover inspiration, techniques & patterns in every issue!

Yes! Rush my FREE issue of *Rug Hooking* Magazine and enter my subscription. If I love it, I'll simply pay the invoice for $37.95* USD for a one year subscription (4 more issues for a total of 5). If I'm not satisfied, I'll return the invoice marked "cancel" and owe absolutely nothing.

SEND NO MONEY NOW-WE'LL BILL YOU LATER

Cut out (or copy) this special coupon and mail to:
Rug Hooking Magazine Subscription Department
PO Box 2263, Williamsport, PA 17703-2263

_____
First Name   Last Name

_____
Postal Address   City   State/Province   Zip/Postal Code

_____
Email Address

* Canadian subscribers add $5/year for S&H + taxes.
Please allow 6-8 weeks for delivery of the first issue.   BWFC20

YOU'RE INVITED TO JOIN THE NEW & IMPROVED BOOK CLUB!

Dear Rug Hooker,

If you love *Rug Hooking* Magazine, then you're going to LOVE our new and improved Book Club! We've refreshed our Book Club with even more benefits so that members can maximize their enjoyment of our rug hooking books. Take a peek at the benefits of becoming a member of the NEW *Rug Hooking* Book Club:

- **Guaranteed discounts on new books**
- **Go green! Hassle-free automatic book payments free from pesky paper invoices or postcards**
- **Exclusive monthly discounts on our online store**
- **Secret sales only for book club members**
- **A free E-Newsletter with book club members-only content**
- **Membership is free! No dues, and no membership fees**

Join the new and improved Book Club today to get interesting, informative books just like these for a guaranteed discount.

  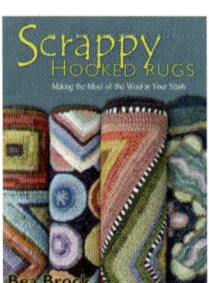 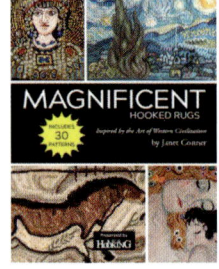 

To learn more about the *Rug Hooking* Book Club and become a Book Club Member today:

 https://www.rughookingmagazine.com/bookclub2020

 877-297-0965 (U.S.)
866-375-8626 (Canada)

Already a Book Club Member?
Click here (or call us) to update your account and access NEW benefits!